101 MUST TRY RECIPES FOR TEENAGE CHEFS

Deliciously Simple & Fun:
101 Teen-Approved Recipes to Cook, Share, and Enjoy - Complete with Easy Tips and Exciting Kitchen Hacks!

Copyright © 2023 di Sam CulinaryKid

All rights reserved

This book is licensed for personal use only.

The book cannot be sold or transferred to third parties.

INTRODUCTION:

Welcome to Your Culinary Adventure!

Hey there, young chefs! Are you ready to become a true kitchen wizard? With "101 Must Try Recipes for Teenage Chefs," you're just steps away from whipping up delicious, fun dishes that are perfect for you, the aspiring culinary enthusiast!

Before we dive in, here are some handy tips to make your cooking experience not only tasty but also safe and organized:

1. The Right Tools: You don't need a professional chef's kitchen! Just some basic utensils like pans, pots, mixing bowls, measuring cups, spoons, kitchen knives (watch those fingers!), a grater, and of course, an oven or a stove. Oh, and don't forget a trusty can opener - you never know!

2. Your Creative Space: Make sure you have enough room to work. A clean and tidy kitchen is your best ally. And if it's small? No worries! A little organization works wonders.

3. Safety First: Remember, safety in the kitchen is key. So, handle knives carefully, be cautious with the heat, and always use oven mitts when grabbing something hot!

4. Clean as You Go: A clean chef is a happy chef! Always wash your hands before you start cooking, and keep your work surfaces clean. And don't forget to clean as you cook – it means less work at the end!

5. Fun is the Main Ingredient: The most important rule? Have fun! The kitchen is a magical place where you can experiment, create, and of course, taste. Don't worry if something doesn't go as planned - every mistake is a learning opportunity.

Now that you're all set, open up this book and let yourself be inspired. Whether it's an energizing breakfast, an afternoon snack, a family dinner, or a party with friends, we have something for every occasion. Get ready to amaze everyone with your new cooking skills!

Tie your apron, it's time to cook!

BREAKFAST

Sunny-Side Up Breakfast Tacos

Ingredients:

- 4 small corn tortillas
- 4 eggs
- 1 avocado, sliced
- 1/2 cup shredded cheddar cheese
- 1 tomato, diced
- 1/4 cup fresh cilantro, chopped
- Salt and pepper, to taste
- Cooking oil or spray

Instructions:

1. **Warm the Tortillas:** Heat a skillet over medium heat. Warm each tortilla for about 30 seconds on each side. Keep them warm by wrapping in a clean towel.
2. **Cook the Eggs:** In the same skillet, add a bit of oil or cooking spray. Crack an egg into the skillet and cook until the white is set but the yolk is still runny, about 2-3 minutes. Repeat with the remaining eggs, adding more oil if needed.
3. **Assemble the Tacos:** Place a warm tortilla on a plate. Add a cooked egg, some avocado slices, a sprinkle of cheese, diced tomato, and a bit of cilantro.
4. **Season and Serve:** Season with a pinch of salt and pepper. Serve immediately for the best taste.

Who says you can't have tacos for breakfast? With these sunny-side up breakfast tacos, every morning can feel like a mini fiesta!

Banana Pancakes

Ingredients:

- 2 ripe bananas
- 1 cup all-purpose flour
- 1 teaspoon baking powder
- 1 egg, lightly beaten
- 1 cup milk
- 1/2 teaspoon vanilla extract
- Pinch of salt
- Butter or cooking oil, for the pan
- Maple syrup and extra banana slices, for serving

Instructions:

1. **Prepare the Batter:** In a large bowl, mash the bananas with a fork until smooth. Add the flour, baking powder, and a pinch of salt. Stir to combine. In another bowl, mix together the beaten egg, milk, and vanilla extract. Pour the wet ingredients into the dry ingredients and stir until just combined. It's okay if there are a few lumps.
2. **Cook the Pancakes:** Heat a non-stick pan or griddle over medium heat and add a little butter or oil. Pour about 1/4 cup of batter for each pancake. Cook until bubbles form on the surface, then flip and cook until golden brown on the other side, about 2 minutes per side.
3. **Serve Hot:** Serve your pancakes hot with maple syrup and extra banana slices on top.

These banana pancakes aren't just a breakfast treat, they're a way to make your morning a-peel-ing! Plus, it's one of the few times you'll get applause for making something go bananas.

Quick Omelette in a Mug

Ingredients:

- 2 eggs
- 2 tablespoons milk
- Salt and pepper, to taste
- 1/4 cup shredded cheese (your choice)
- 1/4 cup diced vegetables (like bell peppers, onions, tomatoes)
- 1 tablespoon cooked ham or bacon, chopped (optional)
- Cooking spray or butter for greasing

Instructions:

1. **Prepare the Mug:** Grease a microwave-safe mug with cooking spray or butter to prevent sticking.
2. **Mix the Ingredients:** In the mug, crack the eggs and add the milk. Beat them together with a fork. Season with salt and pepper. Stir in the cheese, diced vegetables, and, if you're using it, the ham or bacon.
3. **Microwave the Omelette:** Microwave on high for about 1 minute. Stir gently, then microwave for another 30 to 60 seconds, until the eggs are set.
4. **Serve Immediately:** Carefully remove the mug from the microwave (it will be hot!). Enjoy your omelette straight from the mug, or turn it out onto a plate.

This omelette in a mug isn't just a quick breakfast, it's a magic trick in your microwave. Now you see raw eggs, and in a flash, you have a fluffy omelette! It's like having a breakfast genie in a mug.

Yogurt Parfait with Mixed Berries

Ingredients:

- 1 cup Greek yogurt (plain or vanilla flavored)
- 1/2 cup granola
- 1/2 cup mixed berries (like strawberries, blueberries, raspberries)
- 1 tablespoon honey (optional)
- A few mint leaves for garnish (optional)

Instructions:

1. **Layer the Parfait:** In a glass or a jar, start by spooning a layer of Greek yogurt at the bottom.

2. **Add Granola and Berries:** Next, add a layer of granola, followed by a layer of mixed berries.

3. **Repeat Layers:** Continue layering yogurt, granola, and berries until the glass or jar is nearly full. Finish with a final layer of berries on top.

4. **Drizzle with Honey:** If you like a bit of extra sweetness, drizzle honey over the top layer of berries.

5. **Garnish and Serve:** Garnish with a few mint leaves for a fresh touch. Grab a spoon and enjoy!

This yogurt parfait is like a mini treasure hunt in a glass – each spoonful brings a delightful mix of creamy, crunchy, and fruity flavors. It's the fanciest way to eat yogurt and berries, and you get to build it yourself like a delicious masterpiece!

Avocado Toast with Egg

Ingredients:

- 2 slices of whole-grain bread
- 1 ripe avocado
- 2 eggs
- Salt and pepper, to taste
- Optional toppings: cherry tomatoes, radishes, feta cheese, or a sprinkle of chili flakes

Instructions:

1. **Toast the Bread:** Start by toasting the bread slices to your preferred level of crispiness in a toaster or on a skillet.
2. **Prepare the Avocado:** While the bread is toasting, slice the avocado in half, remove the pit, and scoop out the flesh. Mash the avocado with a fork in a bowl, and season it with a pinch of salt and pepper.
3. **Cook the Eggs:** Cook the eggs to your liking. For a sunny-side-up egg, heat a non-stick skillet over medium heat, crack the eggs into the pan, and cook until the whites are set but the yolks are still runny. For scrambled, beat the eggs in a bowl and pour into the skillet, stirring until cooked through.
4. **Assemble the Avocado Toast:** Spread the mashed avocado evenly onto the toasted bread. Gently place the cooked egg on top of the avocado. Add any additional toppings you like.
5. **Serve and Enjoy:** Season with a bit more salt and pepper, or a sprinkle of chili flakes for a kick. Enjoy your trendy and nutritious avocado toast!

Avocado toast isn't just a meal, it's a canvas for your culinary creativity! Experiment with toppings and find your signature style. It's the kind of breakfast that makes you feel like a morning person, even if you're not!

Chocolate Chip Muffins

Ingredients:

- 2 cups all-purpose flour
- 1/2 cup sugar
- 3 teaspoons baking powder
- 1/2 teaspoon salt
- 3/4 cup milk
- 1/3 cup vegetable oil
- 1 egg
- 3/4 cup semi-sweet chocolate chips
- Optional: 1 teaspoon vanilla extract

Instructions:

1. **Preheat and Prepare:** Preheat your oven to 400°F (200°C). Line a muffin tin with paper liners or grease the cups lightly.
2. **Mix Dry Ingredients:** In a large bowl, mix together the flour, sugar, baking powder, and salt.
3. **Add Wet Ingredients:** In another bowl, whisk together the milk, vegetable oil, and egg. If using, add the vanilla extract. Pour the wet ingredients into the dry ingredients and stir until just combined. It's important not to overmix.
4. **Add Chocolate Chips:** Gently fold in the chocolate chips.
5. **Fill Muffin Cups:** Spoon the batter into the prepared muffin cups, filling each about two-thirds full.
6. **Bake the Muffins:** Bake for 20-25 minutes, or until a toothpick inserted into the center of a muffin comes out clean.
7. **Cool and Serve:** Let the muffins cool in the pan for a few minutes, then transfer to a wire rack to cool completely.

> **These chocolate chip muffins are like little bites of happiness. Perfect for a quick breakfast, a school snack, or just when you need a little chocolatey cheer in your day. It's like a smile in a muffin form!**

French Toast Sticks

Ingredients:

- 4 slices of thick bread (like Texas toast or brioche)
- 2 eggs
- 1/2 cup milk
- 1 teaspoon vanilla extract
- 1/2 teaspoon ground cinnamon
- 2 tablespoons sugar
- Butter or oil for cooking
- Maple syrup and powdered sugar, for serving

Instructions:

1. **Prepare the Bread:** Cut each slice of bread into four strips.
2. **Make the Egg Mixture:** In a shallow dish, whisk together the eggs, milk, vanilla extract, cinnamon, and sugar.
3. **Dip the Bread:** Dip each bread strip into the egg mixture, making sure to coat both sides.
4. **Cook the Toast Sticks:** Heat a large skillet or griddle over medium heat. Add butter or oil. Place the dipped bread strips in the skillet. Cook until golden brown on one side, then flip to cook the other side, about 2-3 minutes per side.
5. **Serve Warm:** Serve your French toast sticks warm with maple syrup for dipping and a sprinkle of powdered sugar on top.

French toast sticks are like having dessert for breakfast, but totally acceptable! They're fun to dip, delightful to eat, and make any morning feel like a special occasion. Breakfast just got a whole lot more dunkable!

Homemade Granola with Honey

Ingredients:

- 2 cups old-fashioned oats
- 1/2 cup nuts (almonds, walnuts, or pecans), chopped
- 1/4 cup seeds (sunflower or pumpkin seeds)
- 1/4 cup honey
- 1/4 cup vegetable oil
- 1/2 teaspoon cinnamon
- 1/4 teaspoon salt
- 1/2 cup dried fruits (raisins, cranberries, or chopped apricots)

Instructions:

1. **Preheat the Oven:** Preheat your oven to 300°F (150°C). Line a baking sheet with parchment paper.
2. **Mix Dry Ingredients:** In a large bowl, mix together the oats, nuts, seeds, cinnamon, and salt.
3. **Add Honey and Oil:** Warm the honey slightly to make it easier to stir. Add the honey and vegetable oil to the oat mixture. Stir until everything is well coated.
4. **Bake the Granola:** Spread the granola mixture in an even layer on the prepared baking sheet. Bake for 15-20 minutes, stirring halfway through, until the granola is lightly golden.
5. **Add Dried Fruit:** Once you remove the granola from the oven, stir in the dried fruits while the granola is still warm.
6. **Cool and Store:** Let the granola cool completely on the baking sheet. It will crisp up as it cools. Store in an airtight container.

Making your own granola is like being a magician in the kitchen. A little stirring, a bit of baking, and voilà – you've turned simple oats into a crunchy, golden treasure! It's perfect for breakfast, as a snack, or even as a gift if you can bear to part with it!

Smoothie Bowl with Fresh Fruits

Ingredients:

- 1 cup frozen mixed berries (like strawberries, blueberries, raspberries)
- 1 ripe banana
- 1/2 cup Greek yogurt
- 1/4 cup milk or almond milk
- Toppings: sliced fruits (banana, kiwi, berries), granola, coconut flakes, chia seeds, honey

Instructions:

1. **Blend the Base:** In a blender, combine the frozen berries, banana, Greek yogurt, and milk. Blend until smooth. The mixture should be thick; add a little more milk if necessary, but not too much – you want it spoonable!
2. **Prepare the Bowl:** Pour the smoothie mixture into a bowl.
3. **Add Toppings:** Now the fun part – decorating your bowl! Arrange your chosen toppings on the smoothie base. You can make a pattern or just sprinkle them on top. Drizzle with a bit of honey for extra sweetness.
4. **Serve Immediately:** Enjoy your colorful and nutritious smoothie bowl right away.

A smoothie bowl is like a blank canvas for your breakfast art. Every spoonful is a mix of creamy smoothie and crunchy toppings. It's not just a meal; it's a masterpiece you can eat!

Cheesy Scrambled Eggs

Ingredients:

- 4 eggs
- 1/4 cup milk
- 1/2 cup shredded cheese (cheddar, mozzarella, or your favorite)
- Salt and pepper, to taste
- Butter or oil for cooking
- Optional: chopped herbs (like chives or parsley), diced ham, or chopped vegetables

Instructions:

1. **Beat the Eggs:** In a bowl, beat the eggs with the milk until well mixed. Season with a pinch of salt and pepper.
2. **Cook the Eggs:** Heat a non-stick skillet over medium heat. Add a little butter or oil. Pour in the egg mixture. Let it sit for a moment until it starts to set at the edges.
3. **Add Cheese and Optional Ingredients:** Sprinkle the cheese over the eggs. If using, add your chosen herbs, ham, or vegetables.
4. **Scramble the Eggs:** Gently stir and fold the eggs with a spatula, cooking until they're set but still moist. Avoid overcooking.
5. **Serve Immediately:** Serve the scrambled eggs warm, straight from the skillet.

Cheesy scrambled eggs are like a warm, fluffy cloud in your mouth. Each bite is a cheesy, eggy delight, making mornings a bit more magical. It's like a cheese party, and your taste buds are invited!

Cinnamon Apple Porridge

Ingredients:

- 1 cup rolled oats
- 2 cups milk or water (or a combination of both)
- 1 apple, peeled and diced
- 2 tablespoons brown sugar (or to taste)
- 1/2 teaspoon ground cinnamon
- Pinch of salt
- Optional toppings: chopped nuts, raisins, a drizzle of honey, or a dollop of yogurt

Instructions:

1. **Cook the Oats and Apples:** In a medium saucepan, combine the oats, milk/water, diced apple, brown sugar, cinnamon, and a pinch of salt. Bring to a simmer over medium heat.
2. **Simmer the Porridge:** Cook the mixture, stirring occasionally, for about 5-10 minutes, or until the oats are soft and the porridge has thickened to your liking.
3. **Check the Sweetness:** Taste the porridge and adjust the sweetness if necessary. You can add a little more brown sugar or a drizzle of honey if you like it sweeter.
4. **Serve with Toppings:** Pour the porridge into bowls and add your favorite toppings. Chopped nuts, raisins, a dollop of yogurt, or an extra sprinkle of cinnamon are all great choices.
5. **Enjoy Warm:** Serve the porridge warm for a cozy and comforting breakfast.

This cinnamon apple porridge is like a warm hug in a bowl. It's the perfect way to spice up your morning routine and make getting out of bed a little bit sweeter. Who knew oats could be this exciting?

Bagel with Cream Cheese and Salmon

Ingredients:

- 1 bagel, halved
- 2 tablespoons cream cheese
- 4 slices of smoked salmon
- Fresh dill, for garnish
- Capers (optional)
- Sliced red onion (optional)
- Lemon wedges, for serving
- Salt and pepper, to taste

Instructions:

1. **Toast the Bagel:** Start by toasting the bagel halves until they are lightly crispy on the outside. This can be done in a toaster or oven.
2. **Spread Cream Cheese:** Once the bagel halves are toasted, spread a generous layer of cream cheese on each half.
3. **Add Salmon:** Lay the slices of smoked salmon over the cream cheese. You can fold or layer the salmon in a way that looks appealing.
4. **Add Garnishes:** Sprinkle some fresh dill over the salmon. If you like, add a few capers and some thin slices of red onion for an extra flavor punch.
5. **Season and Serve:** Season with a little bit of salt and pepper to taste. Serve with a wedge of lemon on the side to squeeze over the bagel.
6. **Enjoy:** Enjoy this gourmet-style bagel as a luxurious breakfast or a satisfying brunch.

This bagel with cream cheese and salmon isn't just breakfast, it's a brunch-worthy masterpiece that'll make you feel like you're dining in a fancy café. Talk about starting your day on a high note!

Blueberry Waffles

Ingredients:

- 2 cups all-purpose flour
- 1 tablespoon sugar
- 1 tablespoon baking powder
- 1/2 teaspoon salt
- 2 eggs
- 1 3/4 cups milk
- 1/2 cup vegetable oil or melted butter
- 1 teaspoon vanilla extract
- 1 cup fresh or frozen blueberries
- Butter and maple syrup, for serving

Instructions:

1. **Mix Dry Ingredients:** In a large bowl, whisk together the flour, sugar, baking powder, and salt.
2. **Combine Wet Ingredients:** In another bowl, beat the eggs and then mix in the milk, vegetable oil (or melted butter), and vanilla extract.
3. **Make the Batter:** Pour the wet ingredients into the dry ingredients and stir until just combined. Be careful not to overmix; a few lumps are okay.
4. **Add Blueberries:** Gently fold in the blueberries.
5. **Preheat Waffle Iron:** Heat your waffle iron according to the manufacturer's instructions. Lightly grease it with cooking spray or a little oil.
6. **Cook the Waffles:** Pour enough batter into the waffle iron to just cover the waffle grid. Close the iron and cook until the waffles are golden brown and crisp, usually about 5 minutes.
7. **Serve:** Serve the waffles hot with butter and maple syrup.

These blueberry waffles are like fluffy, crispy clouds with bursts of berry sunshine in every bite. It's like having a little blueberry party in your mouth, and everyone's invited!

Veggie and Cheese Frittata

Ingredients:

- 6 eggs
- 1/2 cup milk
- 1 cup shredded cheese (cheddar, mozzarella, or a mix)
- Salt and pepper, to taste
- 2 tablespoons olive oil
- 1 small onion, finely chopped
- 1 bell pepper, diced
- 1 small zucchini, sliced
- 1 tomato, diced
- Optional: spinach, mushrooms, or any other favorite veggies
- Optional herbs: parsley, basil, or chives, chopped

Instructions:

1. **Preheat the Oven:** Preheat your oven to 375°F (190°C).
2. **Whisk Eggs and Cheese:** In a bowl, whisk together the eggs, milk, half of the shredded cheese, and a pinch of salt and pepper.
3. **Sauté Veggies:** Heat olive oil in an oven-safe skillet over medium heat. Sauté the onion, bell pepper, and zucchini until they are just tender. Add the tomato and any other veggies you're using. Cook for another 2 minutes.
4. **Add Egg Mixture:** Pour the egg and cheese mixture over the sautéed vegetables in the skillet. Let it cook without stirring for about 2 minutes, until the edges start to set.
5. **Bake the Frittata:** Sprinkle the remaining cheese on top and transfer the skillet to the oven. Bake for 10-15 minutes, or until the frittata is set and lightly golden on top.
6. **Garnish and Serve:** Garnish with fresh herbs if desired. Let it cool for a few minutes, then slice and serve.

> **This veggie and cheese frittata is like a veggie party in egg form! Every slice is packed with colors and flavors, making it a perfect way to start your day or to enjoy a simple yet fancy brunch. It's like eating a rainbow for breakfast!**

Peanut Butter and Jelly Oatmeal

Ingredients:

- 1 cup rolled oats
- 2 cups water or milk
- Pinch of salt
- 2 tablespoons peanut butter
- 2 tablespoons jelly or jam of your choice
- Optional toppings: sliced bananas, berries, a sprinkle of cinnamon, or a drizzle of honey

Instructions:

1. **Cook the Oatmeal:** In a saucepan, bring the water or milk to a boil. Add the oats and a pinch of salt. Reduce the heat to medium-low and simmer, stirring occasionally, until the oats are soft and have absorbed the liquid, about 5 minutes.
2. **Add Flavors:** Once the oatmeal is cooked, stir in the peanut butter until it's fully mixed in. Then swirl in the jelly or jam.
3. **Serve:** Spoon the oatmeal into bowls.
4. **Add Toppings:** Top with your choice of additional toppings, like sliced bananas, berries, a sprinkle of cinnamon, or a drizzle of honey.
5. **Enjoy:** Enjoy your warm, comforting bowl of peanut butter and jelly oatmeal.

This peanut butter and jelly oatmeal is like a cozy, warm hug from your favorite childhood sandwich. It's a perfect blend of nutty and sweet, turning a classic duo into a breakfast superstar. It's like starting your day with a PB&J smile!

Breakfast Burritos

Ingredients:

- 4 large flour tortillas
- 6 eggs, beaten
- 1/2 cup shredded cheddar cheese
- 1/2 cup cooked and crumbled sausage or bacon (optional)
- 1/2 cup diced bell peppers
- 1/4 cup diced onions
- Salt and pepper, to taste
- Butter or oil for cooking
- Optional toppings: salsa, sour cream, avocado slices

Instructions:

1. **Cook the Filling:** In a large skillet, heat a bit of butter or oil over medium heat. Add the onions and bell peppers, and cook until softened. Add the beaten eggs, salt, and pepper. Scramble the eggs with the vegetables until just set. If using sausage or bacon, add it now. Sprinkle the cheddar cheese over the eggs and let it melt.
2. **Warm the Tortillas:** Warm the tortillas in a microwave or on a skillet to make them pliable.
3. **Assemble the Burritos:** Lay out the warmed tortillas. Divide the egg and cheese mixture evenly among the tortillas, placing it in a line down the center of each tortilla.
4. **Roll the Burritos:** Fold the sides of each tortilla in, then roll them up from the bottom to enclose the filling.
5. **Optional Grilling:** For a crispy finish, grill the burritos on a hot skillet for a couple of minutes on each side.
6. **Serve with Toppings:** Serve the breakfast burritos with optional toppings like salsa, sour cream, or avocado slices.

These breakfast burritos are like a morning fiesta in your hand! They're a portable, customizable, flavor-packed start to your day. It's like wrapping up the best parts of breakfast in a delicious, edible package!

Homemade Biscuits with Jam

Ingredients for Biscuits:

- 2 cups all-purpose flour
- 1 tablespoon baking powder
- 1 teaspoon sugar
- 1/2 teaspoon salt
- 6 tablespoons cold butter, cut into small pieces
- 3/4 cup milk

Ingredients for Serving:

- Your favorite jam or preserves

Instructions:

1. **Preheat the Oven:** Preheat your oven to 425°F (220°C). Line a baking sheet with parchment paper.
2. **Mix Dry Ingredients:** In a large bowl, whisk together the flour, baking powder, sugar, and salt.
3. **Cut in the Butter:** Add the cold butter pieces to the flour mixture. Using a pastry cutter or your fingers, cut in the butter until the mixture resembles coarse crumbs.
4. **Add Milk:** Pour in the milk and stir just until the dough comes together. Don't overmix.
5. **Form Biscuits:** Turn the dough out onto a lightly floured surface. Gently pat it into a 1-inch thick rectangle. Fold it in half and gently pat it down again. Repeat this folding process 3-4 times (this helps create layers). Then, use a biscuit cutter or a glass to cut out biscuit shapes.
6. **Bake the Biscuits:** Place the biscuits on the prepared baking sheet. Bake for 12-15 minutes, or until they are golden brown on top.
7. **Serve with Jam:** Let the biscuits cool slightly, then split them open and serve with a dollop of your favorite jam.

These homemade biscuits with jam are like little fluffy clouds of happiness. Each bite is a perfect combo of buttery biscuit and sweet, fruity jam. It's like sending your taste buds on a mini-vacation with every bite!

Strawberry Banana Smoothie

Ingredients:

- 1 ripe banana, sliced
- 1 cup fresh or frozen strawberries
- 1/2 cup Greek yogurt
- 1/2 cup milk or almond milk
- 1 tablespoon honey (optional, adjust to taste)
- A few ice cubes (if using fresh strawberries)

Instructions:

1. **Prepare the Ingredients:** If you're using fresh strawberries, wash and hull them. Slice the banana.
2. **Blend the Smoothie:** In a blender, combine the sliced banana, strawberries, Greek yogurt, milk, and honey. If you're using fresh strawberries, add a few ice cubes to the blender.
3. **Blend Until Smooth:** Blend on high speed until the mixture is smooth and creamy. If the smoothie is too thick, you can add a little more milk to reach your desired consistency.
4. **Taste and Adjust:** Give your smoothie a taste. If you'd like it sweeter, you can add a little more honey and blend again.
5. **Serve Immediately:** Pour the smoothie into a glass and enjoy!

This strawberry banana smoothie is like a bright and cheerful start to your day. It's a fruity, creamy delight that's almost like sipping on a liquid sunrise. Perfect for when you need a sweet boost to get moving!

Veggie Hash Browns

Ingredients:

- 2 large potatoes, peeled and grated
- 1 carrot, peeled and grated
- 1 small zucchini, grated
- 1/2 onion, finely chopped
- Salt and pepper, to taste
- 1 egg, beaten
- 2 tablespoons all-purpose flour
- Oil for frying

Instructions:

1. **Drain the Vegetables:** After grating the potatoes, carrot, and zucchini, place them in a clean kitchen towel and squeeze out as much liquid as possible. This will help your hash browns get nice and crispy.
2. **Mix the Ingredients:** In a large bowl, mix together the drained grated vegetables, chopped onion, beaten egg, and flour. Season with salt and pepper.
3. **Form the Hash Browns:** Take a handful of the mixture and form it into a patty. If the mixture doesn't hold together well, you can add a bit more flour.
4. **Fry the Hash Browns:** Heat oil in a large skillet over medium heat. Place the patties in the skillet and flatten them with a spatula. Fry until they are golden brown and crispy, about 4-5 minutes on each side.
5. **Drain and Serve:** Remove the hash browns from the skillet and let them drain on a paper towel. Serve hot.

These veggie hash browns turn ordinary potatoes into a colorful, crispy, veggie-packed feast. It's like eating a rainbow for breakfast – who knew veggies could be this fun and tasty in the morning?

Ham and Cheese Croissant

Ingredients:

- 4 croissants, sliced in half
- 4 slices of ham
- 4 slices of cheese (Swiss, cheddar, or your favorite)
- Mustard or mayonnaise (optional)
- Butter (optional)

Instructions:

1. **Prepare the Croissants:** Preheat your oven to 350°F (175°C). Slice the croissants in half horizontally.
2. **Add Ham and Cheese:** Place a slice of ham and a slice of cheese on the bottom half of each croissant. If you like, spread a little mustard or mayonnaise on the ham before adding the cheese.
3. **Melt the Cheese:** Place the top half of the croissant back on. If desired, you can lightly butter the outside of the croissant for extra crispiness. Put the prepared croissants on a baking sheet.
4. **Bake the Croissants:** Bake in the preheated oven for about 5 minutes, or until the cheese is melted and the croissant is slightly crispy.
5. **Serve Warm:** Serve the ham and cheese croissants warm, right out of the oven.

This ham and cheese croissant is like a mini trip to a Parisian café without leaving your kitchen. It's a simple yet sophisticated way to elevate your breakfast or brunch game. Ooh la la, who knew you could bring a taste of France to your table so easily?

MORNING SNACK

Crispy Apple Nachos

Ingredients:

- 2 large apples, cored and thinly sliced
- 1/4 cup peanut butter, melted
- 1/4 cup chocolate chips, melted
- A handful of granola
- A sprinkle of cinnamon
- Optional toppings: dried cranberries, chopped nuts, mini marshmallows, or coconut flakes

Instructions:

1. **Prepare the Apples:** Core the apples and slice them into thin rounds. Arrange the slices on a large plate or serving platter, overlapping them slightly like nachos.
2. **Drizzle Toppings:** Drizzle the melted peanut butter over the apple slices, followed by the melted chocolate chips. You can microwave the peanut butter and chocolate chips for a few seconds to make them easier to drizzle.
3. **Add Crunch and Flavors:** Sprinkle granola over the apples for a bit of crunch. Add a dash of cinnamon for extra flavor.
4. **Add Additional Toppings:** If you're using any optional toppings like dried cranberries, chopped nuts, mini marshmallows, or coconut flakes, sprinkle them on top.
5. **Serve Immediately:** Enjoy your crispy apple nachos right away while the toppings are still gooey and delicious.

These crispy apple nachos are like a carnival of flavors and textures in every bite. It's a fun, fruity twist on traditional nachos that combines healthy apples with indulgent toppings. Who knew nachos could get a sweet and crunchy makeover like this?

Homemade Granola Bars

Ingredients:

- 2 cups old-fashioned oats
- 1/2 cup nuts (almonds, walnuts, or pecans), chopped
- 1/4 cup honey or maple syrup
- 1/4 cup unsalted butter, melted
- 1/3 cup brown sugar
- 1 teaspoon vanilla extract
- 1/2 teaspoon salt
- 1/2 cup dried fruits (raisins, cranberries, or chopped apricots)
- 1/4 cup mini chocolate chips (optional)

Instructions:

1. **Preheat the Oven:** Preheat your oven to 350°F (175°C). Line an 8-inch square baking pan with parchment paper, leaving some overhang for easy removal.
2. **Toast the Oats and Nuts:** Spread the oats and nuts on a baking sheet. Toast them in the oven for 8-10 minutes, stirring occasionally, until lightly golden.
3. **Melt Butter, Honey, and Sugar:** In a small saucepan over medium heat, combine the butter, honey (or maple syrup), brown sugar, and vanilla extract. Cook, stirring constantly, until the sugar is fully dissolved.
4. **Mix It All Together:** In a large bowl, combine the toasted oats and nuts, melted butter mixture, and salt. Stir until the oats are completely coated. Let it cool for a few minutes, then stir in the dried fruits and chocolate chips, if using.
5. **Press into Pan:** Transfer the granola mixture to the prepared pan. Press it down firmly to ensure it's packed tightly.
6. **Bake the Granola Bars:** Bake for 20-25 minutes, or until the edges turn golden brown.
7. **Cool Completely:** Allow the granola bars to cool completely in the pan. Use the parchment paper overhang to lift them out and cut them into bars or squares.

> **These homemade granola bars are like little treasure bars packed with goodies. They're perfect for a grab-and-go snack or a quick energy boost. And the best part? You made them yourself, so they're extra special!**

Trail Mix

Ingredients:

- 1 cup nuts (almonds, peanuts, walnuts, or a mix)
- 1/2 cup seeds (pumpkin seeds or sunflower seeds)
- 1/2 cup dried fruits (raisins, cranberries, or chopped apricots)
- 1/2 cup pretzels or snack crackers
- 1/4 cup chocolate chips or M&M's (optional)
- A sprinkle of salt (if using unsalted nuts and seeds)
- Optional additions: coconut flakes, popcorn, mini marshmallows

Instructions:

1. **Combine the Ingredients:** In a large bowl, mix together the nuts, seeds, dried fruits, pretzels or snack crackers, and chocolate chips or M&M's, if using. If your nuts and seeds are unsalted, you might want to add a sprinkle of salt.
2. **Toss Well:** Toss everything together until well mixed. This ensures an even distribution of all the ingredients.
3. **Add Optional Extras:** Feel free to get creative and add any other ingredients you love, like coconut flakes, popcorn, or mini marshmallows. Just toss them in with the rest.
4. **Store for Freshness:** Store your trail mix in an airtight container to keep it fresh and crunchy.
5. **Enjoy:** Grab a handful for a quick snack, pack it for a hike, or enjoy it anytime you need a quick energy boost.

Making your own trail mix is like being a snack wizard. You get to conjure up the perfect combination of sweet, salty, crunchy, and chewy. Every handful is a surprise – it's like a party in a bag!

Guacamole and Chips

Ingredients for Guacamole:

- 3 ripe avocados
- 1 small onion, finely chopped
- 1 ripe tomato, diced
- 1 clove garlic, minced
- Juice of 1 lime
- Salt and pepper, to taste
- Optional: chopped cilantro, a diced jalapeño for heat

Ingredients for Chips:

- Corn tortilla chips, for serving

Instructions:

1. **Prepare the Avocados**: Cut the avocados in half, remove the pits, and scoop the flesh into a mixing bowl.
2. **Mash the Avocados:** Use a fork to mash the avocados to your desired consistency, whether you like it chunky or smooth.
3. **Add Flavor:** Add the chopped onion, diced tomato, minced garlic, and lime juice to the mashed avocados. If you're using cilantro or jalapeño, add them now.
4. **Season the Guacamole:** Season with salt and pepper to taste. Mix everything well.
5. **Serve with Chips:** Transfer the guacamole to a serving bowl and surround it with tortilla chips for dipping.
6. **Enjoy:** Dig in and enjoy the creamy, zesty flavors of your homemade guacamole with the crunch of the chips.

Whipping up this guacamole and chips is like bringing a fiesta to your taste buds! It's a simple, fresh, and irresistibly delicious snack that's perfect for sharing – or not, we won't judge!

Peanut Butter Energy Balls

Ingredients:

- 1 cup old-fashioned oats
- 1/2 cup peanut butter
- 1/3 cup honey
- 1/2 cup mini chocolate chips
- 1/2 cup ground flax seeds
- Optional: 1 teaspoon vanilla extract, a pinch of salt, chia seeds, or dried fruit

Instructions:

1. **Combine Ingredients:** In a medium bowl, mix together the oats, peanut butter, honey, chocolate chips, and ground flax seeds. If you're using vanilla extract, a pinch of salt, chia seeds, or dried fruit, add them now.
2. **Chill the Mixture:** Let the mixture chill in the refrigerator for about 30 minutes. This will make it easier to roll into balls.
3. **Form Energy Balls:** Once chilled, roll the mixture into balls about the size of a tablespoon.
4. **Store:** Place the energy balls on a baking sheet or plate and store them in the refrigerator for up to a week, or freeze them for longer storage.
5. **Enjoy:** Grab one as a quick snack, pre-workout energy boost, or a sweet treat.

These peanut butter energy balls are like little bites of superhero fuel. They're packed with energy, easy to make, and perfect for when you need a quick power-up. It's like having a secret snack weapon in your fridge!

Cheese and Fruit Kabobs

Ingredients:

- Your choice of cheese (like cheddar, mozzarella, or gouda), cut into cubes
- A variety of fruits (such as grapes, strawberries, melon balls, and pineapple chunks)
- Wooden skewers

Instructions:

1. **Prepare the Ingredients:** Wash the fruits and cut them into bite-sized pieces if necessary. Cube the cheese into pieces that are easy to skewer.
2. **Assemble the Kabobs:** Start skewering the pieces of fruit and cheese, alternating them for variety and color. For example, you could start with a grape, then add a cube of cheese, followed by a strawberry, and so on.
3. **Arrange the Kabobs:** Once your skewers are filled, arrange them on a platter. You can get creative with the presentation, making a colorful and enticing display.
4. **Serve:** Serve immediately or refrigerate until ready to serve. These kabobs are perfect as a fun snack or a party appetizer.
5. **Enjoy:** Enjoy the delightful combination of sweet fruit and savory cheese in each bite.

These cheese and fruit kabobs are like a party on a stick! They're fun to make, even more fun to eat, and a surefire hit for any gathering. It's like snacking in style!

Hummus and Veggie Sticks

Ingredients for Hummus:

- 1 can (15 oz) chickpeas, drained and rinsed
- 1/4 cup tahini (sesame paste)
- 1 clove garlic
- Juice of 1 lemon
- 2 tablespoons olive oil
- 1/2 teaspoon ground cumin
- Salt and pepper, to taste
- Optional: paprika or chopped parsley for garnish

Ingredients for Veggie Sticks:

- A selection of vegetables such as carrots, celery, bell peppers, and cucumbers, cut into sticks

Instructions:

1. **Make the Hummus:** In a food processor or blender, combine the chickpeas, tahini, garlic, lemon juice, olive oil, cumin, salt, and pepper. Blend until smooth. If the hummus is too thick, you can add a little water or more olive oil to reach your desired consistency.
2. **Taste and Adjust:** Taste the hummus and adjust the seasoning if necessary. You might want to add more lemon juice, garlic, salt, or cumin.
3. **Prepare the Veggie Sticks:** While the hummus is blending, wash and cut your chosen vegetables into stick shapes.
4. **Serve:** Transfer the hummus to a serving bowl. Sprinkle with paprika or chopped parsley, if desired. Arrange the veggie sticks around the bowl or on a separate platter.
5. **Enjoy:** Dip the veggie sticks into the hummus and enjoy a healthy, flavorful snack.

This hummus and veggie sticks combo is like a flavorful journey to the Mediterranean in your own kitchen. It's a healthy, colorful, and delicious way to snack. Plus, you get to say, "I made it myself!" every time you dip a veggie stick!

Greek Yogurt Dip with Veggies

Ingredients for Greek Yogurt Dip:

- 2 cups Greek yogurt
- 1 clove garlic, minced
- 1 tablespoon lemon juice
- 2 tablespoons fresh dill, chopped (or 1 tablespoon dried dill)
- 1 tablespoon fresh parsley, chopped (optional)
- Salt and pepper, to taste
- Olive oil, for drizzling

Ingredients for Veggies:

- A variety of vegetables such as carrots, bell peppers, cucumbers, cherry tomatoes, and broccoli, cut into bite-sized pieces or sticks

Instructions:

1. **Prepare the Dip:** In a medium bowl, combine the Greek yogurt, minced garlic, lemon juice, dill, and parsley if using. Stir well until all the ingredients are incorporated.
2. **Season the Dip:** Add salt and pepper to taste. Give it a good stir to make sure the seasoning is evenly distributed.
3. **Drizzle Olive Oil:** Just before serving, drizzle a little olive oil over the top of the dip for an extra touch of flavor and richness.
4. **Prepare the Vegetables:** While the dip is chilling, wash and cut your chosen vegetables into bite-sized pieces or sticks suitable for dipping.
5. **Serve:** Place the bowl of Greek yogurt dip in the center of a large platter. Arrange the prepared vegetables around the dip.
6. **Enjoy:** Dip your favorite veggies into the creamy, herby yogurt dip and enjoy a healthy, refreshing snack.

This Greek yogurt dip with veggies is like a refreshing dive into a pool on a hot day. It's cool, creamy, and utterly satisfying. Plus, it's a great way to get your daily dose of veggies in a deliciously dip-able form!

Popcorn Mix

Ingredients:

- 1/2 cup popcorn kernels (or 1 bag of microwave popcorn)
- 2 tablespoons butter, melted
- 1/2 teaspoon salt
- 1/4 cup nuts (almonds, peanuts, or cashews)
- 1/4 cup pretzels
- 1/4 cup raisins or dried cranberries
- Optional: 1/4 cup M&M's or chocolate chips

Instructions:

1. **Pop the Corn:** If using popcorn kernels, pop them according to your preferred method (stovetop, air popper, or microwave). If using microwave popcorn, cook it as directed on the package.
2. **Season the Popcorn:** Once popped, transfer the popcorn to a large bowl. Drizzle the melted butter over the popcorn and sprinkle with salt. Toss to coat evenly.
3. **Mix in Extras:** Add the nuts, pretzels, and raisins or dried cranberries to the bowl with the popcorn. Toss everything together to mix.
4. **Add Sweet Treats:** If you're using M&M's or chocolate chips, let the popcorn mix cool slightly before adding them, to prevent them from melting.
5. **Serve and Enjoy:** Once everything is mixed well, serve the popcorn mix in a large bowl or divide it into individual servings.

This popcorn mix is like a mini adventure in every bite. It's a perfect balance of salty, sweet, and crunchy, making it an ideal snack for movie nights, study sessions, or just when you need a little pick-me-up. It's like a party in a bowl!

Baked Sweet Potato Fries

Ingredients:

- 2 large sweet potatoes
- 2 tablespoons olive oil
- 1/2 teaspoon paprika
- 1/2 teaspoon garlic powder
- Salt and pepper, to taste
- Optional: dried herbs like rosemary or thyme

Instructions:

1. **Preheat the Oven:** Preheat your oven to 425°F (220°C). Line a baking sheet with parchment paper.
2. **Prepare the Sweet Potatoes:** Wash and peel the sweet potatoes. Cut them into long, thin strips, about 1/4 inch wide, to resemble fries.
3. **Season the Fries:** In a large bowl, toss the sweet potato strips with olive oil, paprika, garlic powder, and salt and pepper. If you're using dried herbs, add them now.
4. **Arrange on Baking Sheet:** Spread the seasoned sweet potato fries in a single layer on the prepared baking sheet. Make sure they are not overcrowded to ensure even cooking.
5. **Bake the Fries:** Bake in the preheated oven for about 25-30 minutes, turning them once halfway through, until they are golden and crispy.
6. **Serve:** Serve the sweet potato fries hot, with your favorite dipping sauce like ketchup, mayo, or a yogurt-based dip.

These baked sweet potato fries are like little sticks of joy. They're a healthier twist on traditional fries, with a sweet and savory flavor that's utterly addictive. It's like snacking on sunshine!

Mini Caprese Bites

Ingredients:

- Cherry tomatoes, halved
- Mini mozzarella balls (bocconcini)
- Fresh basil leaves
- Balsamic glaze or reduction
- Extra-virgin olive oil
- Salt and pepper, to taste
- Toothpicks

Instructions:

1. **Assemble the Bites:** On a toothpick, skewer a half of a cherry tomato, a basil leaf (folded if large), and a mini mozzarella ball. Repeat this process until you have as many bites as you desire.
2. **Season:** Once assembled, arrange the mini caprese bites on a serving platter. Drizzle them lightly with extra-virgin olive oil and balsamic glaze.
3. **Add Final Touches:** Sprinkle a little salt and pepper over the top to enhance the flavors.
4. **Serve:** Serve immediately as a fresh, tasty appetizer or snack.

These mini caprese bites are like little bursts of Italian sunshine on a toothpick. They're the perfect combination of juicy, creamy, and tangy, making them irresistible. It's like a fancy feast in one bite!

Quesadillas with Cheese and Beans

Ingredients:

- 4 large flour tortillas
- 1 cup shredded cheddar or Monterey Jack cheese
- 1 can (15 oz) black beans, drained and rinsed
- 1/2 teaspoon ground cumin
- Salt and pepper, to taste
- Optional: diced onions, bell peppers, or jalapeños
- Butter or oil for cooking
- Salsa, sour cream, or guacamole for serving

Instructions:

1. **Prepare the Filling:** In a bowl, mix the black beans with ground cumin, salt, and pepper. If you're using onions, bell peppers, or jalapeños, mix them in as well.
2. **Assemble the Quesadillas:** Lay out the tortillas on a flat surface. Sprinkle cheese on one half of each tortilla. Spread the bean mixture over the cheese. Fold the other half of the tortilla over the filling to make a half-moon shape.
3. **Cook the Quesadillas:** Heat a little butter or oil in a skillet over medium heat. Place a quesadilla in the skillet and cook until the bottom is golden brown and crispy, about 2-3 minutes. Flip it over and cook the other side until golden and the cheese is melted.
4. **Serve:** Cut each quesadilla into wedges and serve with salsa, sour cream, or guacamole on the side.

These quesadillas with cheese and beans are like a fiesta in every bite! They're the perfect blend of cheesy, hearty, and crispy – a true comfort food that's also super easy to make. It's like having a little party in your mouth!

Mixed Berry Fruit Salad

Ingredients:

- 1 cup strawberries, hulled and sliced
- 1 cup blueberries
- 1 cup raspberries
- 1 cup blackberries
- 2 tablespoons honey
- Juice of 1 lemon
- Fresh mint leaves for garnish (optional)

Instructions:

1. **Prepare the Berries:** Wash all the berries gently and drain them well. Hull and slice the strawberries. If the other berries are large, you can cut them in half.
2. **Mix Honey and Lemon Juice:** In a small bowl, whisk together the honey and lemon juice until well combined.
3. **Combine Berries and Dressing:** Place all the berries in a large bowl. Pour the honey and lemon mixture over the berries. Gently toss the berries to coat them with the dressing.
4. **Chill and Serve:** Let the fruit salad chill in the refrigerator for about 30 minutes to allow the flavors to meld.
5. **Garnish and Enjoy:** Before serving, garnish with fresh mint leaves for a refreshing touch.

This mixed berry fruit salad is like a bowl of edible jewels – vibrant, sweet, and bursting with flavors. It's a simple yet elegant dessert that's as delightful to look at as it is to eat. Each spoonful is a celebration of summer flavors!

Cucumber Sandwiches

Ingredients:

- 1 cucumber, thinly sliced
- 1 package of cream cheese, softened
- 1/4 cup mayonnaise
- 1 tablespoon fresh dill, chopped (or 1 teaspoon dried dill)
- Salt and pepper, to taste
- Sliced bread (white or whole wheat)
- Optional: lemon zest or juice for added flavor

Instructions:

1. **Prepare the Cream Cheese Mixture:** In a small bowl, mix together the cream cheese, mayonnaise, dill, and a pinch of salt and pepper. If using, add a little lemon zest or juice for an extra zing.
2. **Slice the Cucumbers:** Wash the cucumber and slice it thinly.
3. **Spread Cream Cheese on Bread:** Spread a generous layer of the cream cheese mixture on one side of each slice of bread.
4. **Assemble the Sandwiches:** Lay the cucumber slices over half of the bread slices, on top of the cream cheese layer. Place the remaining bread slices, cream cheese side down, on top of the cucumbers.
5. **Trim and Cut:** Trim the crusts off the sandwiches and then cut each sandwich into small squares or triangles.
6. **Serve:** Arrange the cucumber sandwiches on a platter and serve immediately, or cover and chill until ready to serve.

These cucumber sandwiches are like little bites of elegance. Perfect for a tea party, a light lunch, or just when you're feeling a bit fancy. It's amazing how something so simple can be so delightfully satisfying!

Easy Bruschetta

Ingredients:

- 4 large ripe tomatoes, diced
- 1/4 cup fresh basil leaves, chopped
- 2 cloves garlic, minced
- 1/4 cup extra-virgin olive oil
- 1 tablespoon balsamic vinegar
- Salt and pepper, to taste
- 1 baguette, sliced and toasted
- Optional: grated Parmesan cheese

Instructions:

1. **Make the Tomato Topping:** In a bowl, combine the diced tomatoes, chopped basil, minced garlic, olive oil, and balsamic vinegar. Season with salt and pepper to taste. Let the mixture sit for about 15-30 minutes to allow the flavors to meld together.
2. **Prepare the Baguette**: Preheat your oven to 375°F (190°C). Slice the baguette into 1/2-inch thick rounds. Place the slices on a baking sheet and toast in the oven until lightly golden, about 5-7 minutes.
3. **Assemble the Bruschetta:** Once the bread is toasted, spoon a generous amount of the tomato mixture onto each slice. If you like, sprinkle a little grated Parmesan cheese over the top.
4. **Serve:** Serve the bruschetta immediately while the bread is still warm and crispy.

This easy bruschetta is like a taste of Italy that you can whip up in no time. It's the perfect combination of juicy tomatoes, fresh basil, and crunchy bread. Ideal for impressing guests or treating yourself to a little Mediterranean flair!

Chocolate Covered Strawberries

Ingredients:

- 1 pound fresh strawberries, washed and dried
- 8 ounces semisweet or dark chocolate, chopped
- Optional: White chocolate for drizzling, chopped nuts, or sprinkles for decoration

Instructions:

1. **Prepare the Strawberries:** Ensure the strawberries are completely dry after washing them. Any moisture can cause the chocolate to seize up.
2. **Melt the Chocolate:** Place the chopped chocolate in a heatproof bowl. Melt it in the microwave in 30-second intervals, stirring after each interval, until smooth and fully melted. Alternatively, you can use a double boiler method.
3. **Dip the Strawberries:** Hold a strawberry by the stem and dip it into the melted chocolate, turning it to coat it evenly. Gently shake off any excess chocolate.
4. **Decorate (Optional):** If using, dip the chocolate-covered strawberry into chopped nuts or sprinkles, or drizzle with melted white chocolate.
5. **Set the Strawberries:** Place the dipped strawberries on a baking sheet lined with parchment paper. Repeat with the remaining strawberries.
6. **Chill:** Chill the chocolate-covered strawberries in the refrigerator until the chocolate sets, about 15-30 minutes.
7. **Serve:** Enjoy them as a delightful treat. They're best eaten the same day they are made.

Making chocolate-covered strawberries is like creating edible art – they're as fun to make as they are to eat. They're a luxurious treat that's surprisingly simple to prepare, perfect for special occasions or just because!

Pretzel and Cheese Platter

Ingredients:

- A variety of cheeses (such as cheddar, gouda, brie, and blue cheese), sliced or cubed
- A variety of pretzels (traditional twists, sticks, or flavored varieties)
- Optional additions: sliced cured meats (like salami or prosciutto), nuts, grapes, apple slices, crackers, mustard or honey for dipping

Instructions:

1. **Select the Cheeses:** Choose a variety of cheeses with different textures and flavors. Slice or cube the cheeses for easy snacking.
2. **Prepare the Accompaniments:** If you're including cured meats, roll or fold them for easy serving. Wash and cut any fruits like grapes or apples. Arrange any additional items like nuts or crackers.
3. **Assemble the Platter:** On a large platter or wooden board, begin by placing the cheeses. Then, add the pretzels around and between the cheeses.
4. **Add Variety:** Fill in the gaps with your additional items – cured meats, fruits, nuts, and crackers. This creates a visually appealing and appetizing assortment.
5. **Include Dips:** Place small bowls of mustard, honey, or any other dips you like on the platter.
6. **Serve:** Encourage guests to mix and match their bites, combining the salty pretzels with the various cheeses and accompaniments.

Creating a pretzel and cheese platter is like being an artist with a palette of delicious flavors and textures. It's a fun, interactive way to snack and perfect for gatherings where everyone can find something they love. It's not just a snack; it's a conversation starter!

LUNCH

Easy Mac 'n' Cheese

Ingredients:

- 2 cups elbow macaroni
- 2 tablespoons butter
- 2 tablespoons all-purpose flour
- 2 cups milk
- 2 1/2 cups shredded cheddar cheese
- Salt and pepper, to taste
- Optional: breadcrumbs and a dash of paprika for topping

Instructions:

1. **Cook the Macaroni:** Bring a large pot of salted water to a boil. Add the elbow macaroni and cook according to the package instructions until al dente. Drain and set aside.
2. **Make the Roux:** In the same pot, melt the butter over medium heat. Add the flour and stir constantly for about 1 minute to form a roux. This will thicken the sauce.
3. **Add Milk:** Gradually add the milk to the roux, whisking constantly to prevent lumps. Continue to whisk and cook until the mixture thickens slightly, about 3-5 minutes.
4. **Add Cheese:** Lower the heat and add the shredded cheddar cheese. Stir until the cheese is completely melted and the sauce is smooth.
5. **Combine with Macaroni:** Add the cooked macaroni to the cheese sauce and stir until the macaroni is fully coated.
6. **Season:** Taste and adjust the seasoning with salt and pepper.
7. **Optional Topping:** If using, sprinkle breadcrumbs and a dash of paprika over the top for added texture and flavor.
8. **Serve:** Serve the mac 'n' cheese hot as a comforting and satisfying meal.

This easy mac 'n' cheese is like a warm, cheesy hug in a bowl. It's the ultimate comfort food that brings back delicious childhood memories. Perfect for a quick lunch or whenever you need some cheesy goodness in your life!

Chicken Caesar Salad Wraps

Ingredients:

- 2 cups cooked chicken, shredded or chopped
- 4 large tortillas or wraps
- 2 cups romaine lettuce, chopped
- 1/2 cup Caesar dressing
- 1/2 cup grated Parmesan cheese
- 1/2 cup croutons, lightly crushed
- Salt and pepper, to taste
- Optional: lemon wedges for serving

Instructions:

1. **Prepare the Filling:** In a large bowl, combine the shredded chicken with the Caesar dressing. Mix until the chicken is well coated.
2. **Add Cheese and Lettuce:** Add the chopped romaine lettuce and grated Parmesan cheese to the chicken mixture. Toss everything together until well combined.
3. **Season:** Taste the chicken and lettuce mixture, and season with salt and pepper as needed.
4. **Assemble the Wraps:** Lay out the tortillas or wraps on a flat surface. Divide the chicken and lettuce mixture evenly among the wraps.
5. **Add Croutons:** Sprinkle the crushed croutons over the filling for added crunch.
6. **Roll the Wraps:** Roll up each tortilla tightly, tucking in the sides as you go, to form a wrap.
7. **Cut and Serve:** Cut each wrap in half diagonally and serve immediately. Offer lemon wedges on the side for squeezing over the wraps, if desired.

These chicken Caesar salad wraps are like a delicious, portable feast. They're perfect for a quick lunch, picnic, or a light yet satisfying meal. It's all the flavors of a classic Caesar salad wrapped up in a handy package!

Turkey and Cheese Sandwich

Ingredients:

- Sliced turkey breast (deli style)
- Sliced cheese of your choice (cheddar, Swiss, or provolone)
- 2 slices of bread (whole grain, white, or sourdough)
- Lettuce leaves
- Tomato slices
- Mayonnaise or mustard
- Salt and pepper, to taste

Instructions:

1. **Toast the Bread:** If you prefer, lightly toast the bread slices for added texture and flavor.
2. **Spread Mayo or Mustard:** Spread mayonnaise or mustard on one side of each slice of bread.
3. **Add Turkey and Cheese:** Layer the sliced turkey and cheese on one slice of bread.
4. **Add Veggies:** Place lettuce leaves and tomato slices on top of the cheese. Season the tomato slices with a little salt and pepper.
5. **Close the Sandwich:** Place the second slice of bread on top, mayo or mustard side down.
6. **Cut and Serve:** Cut the sandwich in half or into quarters, depending on your preference.

This turkey and cheese sandwich is a classic, no-fuss lunch option that's both satisfying and easy to make. It's like having a deli in your own kitchen - simple, tasty, and always a good idea!

Veggie-Packed Pasta Salad

Ingredients:

- 2 cups pasta (like penne, fusilli, or rotini)
- 1 cup cherry tomatoes, halved
- 1 cup cucumber, diced
- 1 bell pepper, diced
- 1/2 cup red onion, finely chopped
- 1/2 cup olives, sliced
- 1/2 cup feta cheese, crumbled
- 1/4 cup fresh basil, chopped
- 1/4 cup olive oil
- 2 tablespoons balsamic vinegar or red wine vinegar
- 1 garlic clove, minced
- Salt and pepper, to taste

Instructions:

1. **Cook the Pasta:** Bring a large pot of salted water to a boil. Add the pasta and cook according to package instructions until al dente. Drain and rinse under cold water to cool.
2. **Prepare the Dressing:** In a small bowl, whisk together the olive oil, vinegar, minced garlic, salt, and pepper.
3. **Combine Pasta and Veggies:** In a large bowl, combine the cooled pasta, cherry tomatoes, cucumber, bell pepper, red onion, and olives.
4. **Add Dressing:** Pour the dressing over the pasta and veggies and toss well to coat everything evenly.
5. **Add Cheese and Basil:** Gently mix in the crumbled feta cheese and fresh basil.
6. **Chill and Serve:** Let the pasta salad chill in the refrigerator for at least 30 minutes before serving. This allows the flavors to meld together.

This veggie-packed pasta salad is like a rainbow in a bowl - colorful, fresh, and full of flavor. It's perfect for picnics, potlucks, or as a refreshing side dish on a warm day. Each forkful is a delightful bite of summery goodness!

Simple Tomato Soup with Grilled Cheese

Ingredients for Tomato Soup:

- 2 tablespoons olive oil
- 1 onion, chopped
- 2 garlic cloves, minced
- 1 can (28 oz) crushed tomatoes
- 2 cups vegetable or chicken broth
- 1 teaspoon sugar
- Salt and pepper, to taste
- Optional: basil or oregano for seasoning

Ingredients for Grilled Cheese:

- 4 slices of bread
- 2 tablespoons butter, softened
- 4 slices of cheese (cheddar, American, or your favorite)

Instructions:

1. **Cook the Onion and Garlic**: In a large pot, heat the olive oil over medium heat. Add the chopped onion and minced garlic, and sauté until the onion is translucent.
2. **Add Tomatoes and Broth:** Pour in the crushed tomatoes and broth. Stir to combine.
3. **Season the Soup:** Add sugar, salt, and pepper to the soup. If using, add basil or oregano. Bring the mixture to a simmer.
4. **Simmer:** Let the soup simmer for about 20 minutes, stirring occasionally.
5. **Prepare Grilled Cheese:** While the soup is simmering, butter one side of each bread slice. Place a slice of cheese between two slices of bread, with the buttered sides facing out.
6. **Cook Grilled Cheese:** Heat a skillet over medium heat. Place the sandwich in the skillet and cook until golden brown on one side, then flip and cook the other side until golden and the cheese is melted.
7. **Blend the Soup (Optional):** For a smoother soup, use an immersion blender or stand blender to puree the soup until smooth.
8. **Serve:** Ladle the tomato soup into bowls and serve with the warm grilled cheese sandwich.

> **Fun Tip: This simple tomato soup with grilled cheese is the ultimate comfort food duo. Dipping a crispy, gooey grilled cheese into a bowl of warm, velvety tomato soup is like a cozy embrace for your taste buds. Perfect for a comforting meal any day!**

BLT Sandwich

Ingredients:

- 4 slices of bacon
- 2 slices of bread (toasted if desired)
- Lettuce leaves
- 2-3 slices of ripe tomato
- Mayonnaise
- Salt and pepper, to taste

Instructions:

1. **Cook the Bacon:** In a skillet, cook the bacon over medium heat until it's crispy. Drain the bacon on paper towels to remove excess grease.
2. **Prepare the Toast:** If you prefer your sandwich with a crunch, toast the bread slices to your desired level of crispiness.
3. **Spread Mayonnaise:** Spread a generous layer of mayonnaise on one side of each slice of bread.
4. **Assemble the Sandwich:** On one slice of bread, lay the lettuce leaves, followed by the tomato slices. Season the tomato with a pinch of salt and pepper.
5. **Add Bacon:** Place the cooked bacon on top of the tomato slices.
6. **Close the Sandwich:** Top with the second slice of bread, mayonnaise side down.
7. **Cut and Serve:** Cut the sandwich in half diagonally and serve immediately.

The BLT sandwich is a classic that never goes out of style. It's a perfect blend of crunchy, savory, and fresh flavors. Each bite is a delightful mix of crispy bacon, juicy tomato, and crisp lettuce - simple yet incredibly satisfying!

Chicken Quesadillas

Ingredients:

- 2 cups cooked chicken, shredded
- 4 large flour tortillas
- 1 cup shredded cheese (cheddar, Monterey Jack, or a mix)
- 1/2 cup onion, finely chopped
- 1/2 cup bell pepper, diced
- 1 clove garlic, minced
- 1 teaspoon chili powder
- Salt and pepper, to taste
- Olive oil or butter for cooking
- Optional: salsa, sour cream, or guacamole for serving

Instructions:

1. **Prepare the Filling:** In a bowl, combine the shredded chicken with chili powder, salt, and pepper. Mix well.
2. **Cook Onion and Pepper:** In a skillet, heat a little olive oil or butter. Add the chopped onion and bell pepper, and cook until they are soft. Add the minced garlic and cook for another minute.
3. **Assemble the Quesadillas:** Lay out the tortillas on a flat surface. Sprinkle cheese on one half of each tortilla. Top the cheese with the chicken mixture and the cooked onion and pepper.
4. **Cook the Quesadillas:** Fold the other half of the tortilla over the filling. Heat a clean skillet over medium heat and cook each quesadilla until golden brown on one side, then flip and cook until the other side is golden brown and the cheese is melted.
5. **Serve:** Cut the quesadillas into wedges and serve with salsa, sour cream, or guacamole if desired.

Chicken quesadillas are a quick and delicious meal that's always a crowd-pleaser. They're like a warm, cheesy, and flavorful hug in every bite. Perfect for a casual dinner or when you need a tasty snack that satisfies!

Tuna Salad Sandwich

Ingredients:

- 1 can (5 oz) tuna, drained
- 2 tablespoons mayonnaise
- 1 tablespoon Dijon mustard
- 1/4 cup celery, finely chopped
- 1 tablespoon red onion, finely chopped
- 1 tablespoon lemon juice
- Salt and pepper, to taste
- Lettuce leaves
- Slices of tomato
- 4 slices of bread
- Optional: pickles, cucumber slices, or sprouts

Instructions:

1. **Make the Tuna Salad:** In a bowl, mix together the drained tuna, mayonnaise, Dijon mustard, chopped celery, chopped red onion, and lemon juice. Season with salt and pepper to taste.
2. **Toast the Bread:** If you prefer a crispy texture, lightly toast the bread slices.
3. **Assemble the Sandwich:** Spread the tuna salad evenly on two slices of bread. Add lettuce leaves and tomato slices on top of the tuna. If desired, add pickles, cucumber slices, or sprouts for extra crunch and flavor.
4. **Close the Sandwich:** Top with the remaining slices of bread.
5. **Cut and Serve:** Cut the sandwiches in half or quarters, depending on your preference.

A tuna salad sandwich is a classic lunchtime favorite that's both satisfying and easy to whip up. It's a perfect blend of creamy, crunchy, and tangy flavors, making it a delightful meal that's ready in minutes!

Veggie Stir Fry with Rice

Ingredients:

- 2 cups cooked rice
- 2 tablespoons vegetable oil
- 1 bell pepper, sliced
- 1 carrot, julienned
- 1 cup broccoli florets
- 1/2 cup snap peas
- 2 cloves garlic, minced
- 2 tablespoons soy sauce
- 1 tablespoon sesame oil
- Salt and pepper, to taste
- Optional: sesame seeds, green onions for garnish

Instructions:

1. Heat vegetable oil in a large skillet or wok over medium-high heat. Add garlic, bell pepper, carrot, broccoli, and snap peas. Stir-fry until vegetables are tender-crisp.
2. Add cooked rice, soy sauce, and sesame oil to the skillet. Stir to combine and heat through.
3. Season with salt and pepper. Garnish with sesame seeds and green onions if desired.

This veggie stir fry with rice is like a colorful canvas of flavors and textures. Each forkful is a delightful journey through crisp vegetables and comforting rice, proving that eating your veggies can be both delicious and fun!

Homemade Pizza Bagels

Ingredients:

- 4 bagels, halved
- 1 cup pizza sauce
- 2 cups shredded mozzarella cheese
- Toppings: pepperoni, mushrooms, bell peppers, olives
- Italian seasoning, to taste

Instructions:

1. Preheat oven to 375°F (190°C). Place bagel halves on a baking sheet.
2. Spread pizza sauce on each bagel half. Sprinkle with cheese.
3. Add your favorite toppings and a dash of Italian seasoning.
4. Bake for 10-15 minutes or until cheese is melted and bubbly.

Turning bagels into mini pizzas is like hosting a tiny Italian feast right in your kitchen. It's a playful twist on pizza night that lets everyone become a chef, creating their own delicious masterpiece on a bagel!

Beef and Cheese Tacos

Ingredients:

- 1 lb ground beef
- Taco seasoning packet
- 8-10 taco shells
- 1 cup shredded cheddar cheese
- Lettuce, tomatoes, and sour cream for garnish

Instructions:

1. Cook ground beef in a skillet over medium heat until browned. Drain excess grease.
2. Stir in taco seasoning and cook according to package instructions.
3. Warm taco shells as directed on package.
4. Fill each taco shell with beef, top with cheese, lettuce, and tomatoes.
5. Serve with a dollop of sour cream.

These beef and cheese tacos bring the fiesta to your taste buds. Every bite is a mix of savory beef, melty cheese, and fresh toppings, wrapped up in a crunchy shell – it's like a party in every bite!

Egg Salad Sandwich

Ingredients:

- 6 hard-boiled eggs, chopped
- 1/4 cup mayonnaise
- 1 tablespoon mustard
- Salt and pepper, to taste
- Lettuce and bread for serving

Instructions:

1. In a bowl, mix chopped eggs, mayonnaise, mustard, salt, and pepper.
2. Spread egg salad on a slice of bread, add lettuce, top with another slice of bread.
3. Cut sandwich in half and serve.

The classic egg salad sandwich is like a comforting hug in sandwich form. Each bite is a creamy, eggy delight, perfect for a quick lunch or picnic. It's a simple yet satisfying way to enjoy the humble egg!

Chicken Noodle Soup

Ingredients:

- 1 tablespoon olive oil
- 1 onion, chopped
- 2 carrots, sliced
- 2 celery stalks, sliced
- 1 lb chicken breast, cubed
- 6 cups chicken broth
- 1 cup egg noodles
- Salt and pepper, to taste
- Optional: parsley for garnish

Instructions:

1. In a large pot, heat olive oil over medium heat. Add onion, carrots, and celery. Cook until softened.
2. Add chicken and cook until no longer pink.
3. Pour in chicken broth and bring to a boil. Reduce heat, add noodles, and simmer until noodles are tender.
4. Season with salt and pepper. Garnish with parsley if desired.

This chicken noodle soup is like a warm embrace on a chilly day. With tender chicken, comforting noodles, and a rich broth, it's a soothing remedy for the soul and a classic comfort food that never goes out of style.

Veggie Burgers

Ingredients:

- 1 can (15 oz) black beans, drained and rinsed
- 1/2 cup breadcrumbs
- 1/4 cup grated carrots
- 1/4 cup finely chopped bell pepper
- 2 green onions, finely chopped
- 1 egg
- 1 teaspoon garlic powder
- 1 teaspoon onion powder
- Salt and pepper, to taste
- 1 tablespoon olive oil
- 4 burger buns
- Lettuce, tomato, and condiments for serving

Instructions:

1. **Mash the Beans:** In a bowl, mash the black beans with a fork until mostly smooth.
2. **Make the Burger Mixture:** To the mashed beans, add the breadcrumbs, grated carrots, chopped bell pepper, green onions, egg, garlic powder, onion powder, salt, and pepper. Mix until well combined.
3. **Form the Patties:** Divide the mixture into four equal portions and shape each into a burger patty.
4. **Cook the Burgers:** Heat olive oil in a skillet over medium heat. Cook the patties for about 4-5 minutes on each side, until they are heated through and have a nice crust.
5. **Assemble the Burgers:** Place each patty on a bun and top with lettuce, tomato, and your favorite condiments.
6. **Serve:** Serve the veggie burgers immediately, with additional toppings on the side if desired.

These veggie burgers are a delightful twist on the classic burger. They're packed with flavor and wholesome ingredients, making them not just tasty but also a guilt-free pleasure. Perfect for a summer barbecue or a casual dinner, they're a sure way to impress both vegetarians and meat-eaters alike!

Cheese and Tomato Panini

Ingredients:

- 4 slices of Italian bread or ciabatta
- 4 slices of mozzarella cheese
- 1 tomato, thinly sliced
- Fresh basil leaves
- 2 tablespoons olive oil
- Salt and pepper, to taste
- Optional: balsamic glaze for drizzling

Instructions:

1. **Assemble the Panini:** Lay out two slices of bread. On each slice, place two slices of mozzarella cheese, a few slices of tomato, and a couple of basil leaves. Season the tomato with a pinch of salt and pepper. Top with the remaining bread slices.
2. **Brush with Olive Oil:** Lightly brush the outside of each sandwich with olive oil.
3. **Heat the Panini Press:** Preheat your Panini press or a skillet over medium heat.
4. **Cook the Panini:** Place the sandwiches in the Panini press or on the skillet. If using a skillet, press down with a spatula and flip halfway through to ensure even cooking. Cook until the bread is golden and crispy, and the cheese has melted.
5. **Optional Balsamic Glaze:** Drizzle a bit of balsamic glaze over the Panini for added flavor.
6. **Serve:** Slice the Panini in half and serve hot.

This cheese and tomato Panini is like a little slice of Italian heaven. The crispy bread, melted cheese, fresh tomato, and basil come together in a symphony of flavors. It's a gourmet lunch made easy, perfect for a quick yet impressive meal!

Shrimp Fried Rice

Ingredients:

- 1 pound shrimp, peeled and deveined
- 2 cups cooked rice (preferably leftover or day-old)
- 2 tablespoons vegetable oil
- 2 eggs, beaten
- 1 cup frozen peas and carrots, thawed
- 1 small onion, diced
- 2 cloves garlic, minced
- 3 tablespoons soy sauce
- 1 tablespoon sesame oil
- Salt and pepper, to taste
- Optional: green onions and sesame seeds for garnish

Instructions:

1. **Cook the Shrimp:** In a skillet or wok, heat 1 tablespoon of vegetable oil over medium-high heat. Add the shrimp, season with salt and pepper, and cook until pink and opaque, about 2-3 minutes per side. Remove shrimp from the skillet and set aside.
2. **Scramble the Eggs:** In the same skillet, add the beaten eggs and scramble until just set. Remove the eggs and set aside.
3. **Sauté Vegetables:** Add another tablespoon of oil to the skillet. Sauté the diced onion and minced garlic until the onion is translucent. Add the peas and carrots and cook until they are heated through.
4. **Combine Ingredients:** Add the cooked rice to the skillet with the vegetables. Stir to combine.
5. **Season the Rice:** Pour soy sauce and sesame oil over the rice. Stir until the rice is evenly coated with the sauce.
6. **Add Shrimp and Eggs:** Return the cooked shrimp and scrambled eggs to the skillet. Stir to mix them into the rice.
7. **Serve:** Taste and adjust seasoning with salt and pepper if needed. Serve the shrimp fried rice hot, garnished with green onions and sesame seeds if desired.

> **This shrimp fried rice is a savory, satisfying dish that brings a touch of Asian flair to your dining table. It's a perfect way to turn leftover rice into an exotic and delicious meal. Every bite is filled with flavorful shrimp and colorful veggies – a feast for both your eyes and your palate!**

Chicken Alfredo Pasta

Ingredients:

- 2 boneless, skinless chicken breasts
- Salt and pepper, to taste
- 2 tablespoons olive oil
- 8 oz fettuccine pasta
- 1 cup heavy cream
- 1/2 cup unsalted butter
- 1 cup grated Parmesan cheese
- 2 cloves garlic, minced
- Optional: parsley for garnish

Instructions:

1. **Season and Cook Chicken:** Season the chicken breasts with salt and pepper. In a skillet, heat the olive oil over medium heat. Cook the chicken until golden brown and cooked through, about 5-7 minutes per side. Remove from skillet and slice.
2. **Cook the Pasta:** Cook the fettuccine according to package instructions in salted water until al dente. Drain, reserving some of the pasta water.
3. **Make Alfredo Sauce:** In the same skillet, melt the butter over medium heat. Add the minced garlic and cook for about 1 minute. Pour in the heavy cream and bring to a simmer. Stir in the grated Parmesan cheese until it melts and the sauce thickens.
4. **Combine Pasta and Sauce:** Add the cooked pasta to the Alfredo sauce, tossing to coat. If the sauce is too thick, use the reserved pasta water to thin it to your desired consistency.
5. **Add Chicken:** Add the cooked, sliced chicken to the pasta and toss to combine.
6. **Serve:** Serve the chicken Alfredo pasta hot, garnished with parsley if desired.

Chicken Alfredo pasta is like a creamy, dreamy Italian delight in every bite. The rich sauce, tender chicken, and perfectly cooked pasta come together for a truly indulgent experience. It's a classic dish that feels fancy yet is surprisingly easy to make at home!

Bean and Cheese Burritos

Ingredients:

- 1 can (15 oz) refried beans
- 4 large flour tortillas
- 1 cup shredded cheddar or Monterey Jack cheese
- 1/2 cup salsa
- 1/4 cup onion, finely chopped
- 1/4 cup green bell pepper, diced
- 1 teaspoon chili powder
- Salt to taste
- Optional: sour cream, guacamole, lettuce, and diced tomato for serving

Instructions:

1. **Prepare the Bean Mixture:** In a bowl, mix together the refried beans, chili powder, salt, chopped onion, and diced bell pepper.
2. **Heat the Tortillas:** Warm the tortillas in a microwave or on a skillet to make them more pliable.
3. **Assemble the Burritos:** Lay out the tortillas on a flat surface. Spread a quarter of the bean mixture onto the center of each tortilla. Top with salsa and a sprinkle of cheese.
4. **Roll the Burritos:** Fold the sides of the tortilla over the filling, then roll from the bottom up to enclose the filling and form a burrito.
5. **Cook the Burritos:** Heat a skillet over medium heat. Place the burritos seam side down and cook until golden brown and crispy, about 2 minutes per side.
6. **Serve:** Cut the burritos in half and serve with optional toppings like sour cream, guacamole, lettuce, and diced tomato.

Bean and cheese burritos are a simple yet satisfying meal that's perfect for any time of the day. They're like a cozy, flavorful wrap filled with creamy beans and melty cheese, making them a hit for both quick dinners and on-the-go lunches. It's comfort food that's both delicious and easy to make!

Caesar Salad with Croutons

Ingredients:

- 1 head of romaine lettuce, chopped
- 1/2 cup grated Parmesan cheese
- 1 cup croutons
- Caesar dressing (store-bought or homemade)
- 1 clove garlic, minced (for homemade dressing)
- 2 anchovy fillets, mashed (optional for homemade dressing)
- 1/3 cup olive oil (for homemade dressing)
- 2 tablespoons lemon juice (for homemade dressing)
- 1 teaspoon Dijon mustard (for homemade dressing)
- Salt and pepper, to taste
- Optional: grilled chicken or shrimp for a protein boost

Instructions:

1. **Prepare the Lettuce:** Wash and chop the romaine lettuce into bite-sized pieces. Place in a large salad bowl.
2. **Make the Dressing:** If making homemade dressing, combine minced garlic, mashed anchovies (if using), olive oil, lemon juice, Dijon mustard, salt, and pepper in a bowl. Whisk until well combined. Alternatively, use your favorite store-bought Caesar dressing.
3. **Toss the Salad:** Drizzle the Caesar dressing over the lettuce in the bowl. Toss until the lettuce is evenly coated with the dressing.
4. **Add Cheese and Croutons:** Sprinkle the grated Parmesan cheese and croutons over the salad. Toss lightly again.
5. **Optional Protein:** If desired, add grilled chicken or shrimp on top of the salad for added protein.
6. **Serve:** Serve the Caesar salad immediately, offering additional Parmesan cheese and croutons on the side if desired.

This Caesar salad with croutons brings a classic touch to any meal. The crisp lettuce, creamy dressing, and crunchy croutons create a harmony of textures and flavors that's both refreshing and indulgent. It's like a timeless symphony for your taste buds!

Pita Bread with Tzatziki

Ingredients for Tzatziki:

- 1 cup Greek yogurt
- 1 cucumber, grated and drained
- 2 cloves garlic, minced
- 2 tablespoons olive oil
- 1 tablespoon lemon juice
- 1 tablespoon fresh dill, chopped (or 1 teaspoon dried dill)
- Salt and pepper, to taste

Ingredients for Serving:

- Pita bread, warmed

Instructions:

1. **Prepare the Tzatziki:** In a medium bowl, combine Greek yogurt, grated and drained cucumber, minced garlic, olive oil, lemon juice, and dill. Mix well.
2. **Season the Tzatziki:** Add salt and pepper to taste. Stir the tzatziki sauce until all ingredients are well combined.
3. **Chill:** For the best flavor, cover and refrigerate the tzatziki for at least 30 minutes before serving. This allows the flavors to meld together.
4. **Serve with Pita Bread: Warm** the pita bread in the oven or on a skillet. Cut into wedges or strips for easy dipping.
5. **Enjoy:** Serve the tzatziki sauce with the warm pita bread for dipping.

This pita bread with tzatziki is like taking a quick culinary trip to the Mediterranean. The cool, creamy tzatziki paired with warm, fluffy pita is a match made in heaven, perfect for a light snack, appetizer, or part of a meze platter. It's a simple yet sophisticated treat that's sure to impress!

AFTERNOON SNACK

Fruit and Yogurt Smoothie

Ingredients:

- 1 cup mixed frozen fruits (such as berries, mango, or pineapple)
- 1 ripe banana
- 1/2 cup Greek yogurt
- 1/2 cup milk or a milk alternative
- 1 tablespoon honey or maple syrup (optional)
- A few ice cubes (if using fresh fruit)

Instructions:

1. **Prepare the Ingredients:** If you're using fresh fruit instead of frozen, prepare it by washing and cutting it into smaller pieces. Peel the banana.
2. **Blend the Smoothie:** In a blender, combine the mixed fruits, banana, Greek yogurt, milk, and honey or maple syrup if you're using it. If you're using fresh fruit, add a few ice cubes to the blender.
3. **Blend Until Smooth:** Blend on high speed until the mixture is smooth and creamy. If the smoothie is too thick, you can add a little more milk to reach your desired consistency.
4. **Taste and Adjust:** Give your smoothie a taste. If you'd like it sweeter, you can add a little more honey or maple syrup and blend again.
5. **Serve Immediately:** Pour the smoothie into a glass and enjoy!

This fruit and yogurt smoothie is like a refreshing rainbow in a glass – vibrant, nutritious, and bursting with flavors. It's a perfect way to start your day, energize your afternoon, or cool down after a workout. Each sip is a delicious blend of your favorite fruits and creamy yogurt!

Avocado and Tomato Salsa

Ingredients:

- 2 ripe avocados, diced
- 2 medium tomatoes, diced
- 1/4 cup red onion, finely chopped
- 1 jalapeño pepper, seeded and minced (optional)
- Juice of 1 lime
- 2 tablespoons fresh cilantro, chopped
- Salt and pepper, to taste

Instructions:

1. **Prepare the Ingredients**: Dice the avocados and tomatoes into small, bite-sized pieces. Finely chop the red onion and cilantro. If using, mince the jalapeño pepper, making sure to remove the seeds if you want to reduce the heat.
2. **Combine the Salsa:** In a medium bowl, gently mix together the diced avocados, tomatoes, red onion, jalapeño (if using), and chopped cilantro.
3. **Add Lime Juice and Season:** Squeeze the juice of one lime over the salsa. Add salt and pepper to taste. Gently toss everything together to combine.
4. **Chill:** For the best flavor, let the salsa chill in the refrigerator for about 30 minutes before serving. This allows the flavors to meld together.
5. **Serve:** Serve the avocado and tomato salsa with tortilla chips, as a topping for tacos, or with grilled meats or fish.

This avocado and tomato salsa is like a fiesta in a bowl – vibrant, fresh, and full of zesty flavors. It's a perfect snack for sharing and adds a burst of color and taste to any dish. Dive in with your favorite chips and enjoy the creamy avocado and juicy tomatoes in every scoop!

Cheesy Garlic Breadsticks

Ingredients:

- 1 pre-made pizza dough or French bread dough
- 4 tablespoons unsalted butter, melted
- 2 cloves garlic, minced
- 1 teaspoon Italian seasoning
- 1 cup shredded mozzarella cheese
- 1/4 cup grated Parmesan cheese
- Optional: marinara sauce for dipping

Instructions:

1. **Prepare the Dough:** Preheat your oven to 375°F (190°C). If using pizza dough, roll it out into a rectangle on a floured surface. If using French bread dough, slice it in half lengthwise.
2. **Make Garlic Butter:** In a small bowl, combine the melted butter with minced garlic and Italian seasoning.
3. **Apply Garlic Butter:** Brush the garlic butter generously over the surface of the dough.
4. **Add Cheese:** Sprinkle the shredded mozzarella and grated Parmesan cheese evenly over the dough.
5. **Bake:** Place the dough on a baking sheet. Bake in the preheated oven for 12-15 minutes or until the cheese is melted and bubbly and the edges are golden brown.
6. **Slice:** Remove from the oven and let it cool for a few minutes. Cut into strips to create breadsticks.
7. **Serve:** Serve warm, optionally with marinara sauce for dipping.

These cheesy garlic breadsticks are a mouth-watering treat that's impossible to resist. They're the perfect blend of gooey cheese, aromatic garlic, and soft, warm bread – a sure hit whether you're snacking solo or sharing with friends. Each bite is a little piece of cheesy heaven!

Baked Mozzarella Sticks

Ingredients:

- 12 mozzarella cheese sticks
- 1/2 cup all-purpose flour
- 2 eggs, beaten
- 1 cup breadcrumbs
- 1 teaspoon garlic powder
- 1 teaspoon Italian seasoning
- Salt and pepper, to taste
- Cooking spray

Instructions:

1. **Freeze the Cheese:** Unwrap the mozzarella sticks and place them in the freezer for at least an hour. This helps them keep their shape while baking.
2. **Preheat the Oven:** Preheat your oven to 400°F (200°C). Line a baking sheet with parchment paper.
3. **Dredge the Cheese:** Create a dredging station with three bowls – one with flour, one with beaten eggs, and one with breadcrumbs mixed with garlic powder, Italian seasoning, salt, and pepper.
4. **Coat the Cheese:** Roll each frozen cheese stick in the flour, then dip in the egg, and finally coat with the breadcrumb mixture. Press the breadcrumbs onto the cheese stick to ensure a good coating.
5. **Arrange on Baking Sheet:** Place the coated cheese sticks on the prepared baking sheet. Spray them lightly with cooking spray. This helps achieve a golden color.
6. **Bake:** Bake in the preheated oven for about 8-10 minutes or until the cheese sticks are crispy and golden brown. Keep an eye on them to make sure they don't melt completely.
7. **Serve:** Let the mozzarella sticks cool for a few minutes before serving. Serve with marinara sauce or ranch dressing for dipping.

These baked mozzarella sticks are a guilt-free indulgence that's just as satisfying as their fried counterpart. They're the perfect snack for cheese lovers – crispy on the outside, gooey on the inside, and utterly delicious. Dip them in your favorite sauce and enjoy the melty, cheesy goodness!

Oatmeal Raisin Cookies

Ingredients:

- 1 cup all-purpose flour
- 1 1/2 cups rolled oats
- 1/2 teaspoon baking soda
- 1/2 teaspoon cinnamon
- 1/4 teaspoon salt
- 1/2 cup unsalted butter, softened
- 1/2 cup brown sugar
- 1/4 cup granulated sugar
- 1 egg
- 1 teaspoon vanilla extract
- 3/4 cup raisins

Instructions:

1. **Dry Ingredients:** In a medium bowl, whisk together the flour, rolled oats, baking soda, cinnamon, and salt.
2. **Cream Butter and Sugars:** In a large bowl, beat the softened butter with the brown sugar and granulated sugar until creamy. Add the egg and vanilla extract, continuing to beat until well combined.
3. **Combine Mixtures:** Gradually add the dry ingredients to the wet ingredients, mixing until just combined.
4. **Add Raisins:** Stir in the raisins until evenly distributed throughout the dough.
5. Chill the Dough: Cover the dough and refrigerate for at least 30 minutes. This helps the cookies hold their shape while baking.
6. **Preheat the Oven:** Preheat your oven to 350°F (175°C). Line a baking sheet with parchment paper.
7. **Form Cookies:** Using a spoon or cookie scoop, drop rounded balls of dough onto the prepared baking sheet. Leave enough space between each cookie for expansion.
8. **Bake:** Bake for 10-12 minutes or until the cookies are golden brown around the edges but still soft in the center.
9. **Cool:** Allow the cookies to cool on the baking sheet for a few minutes before transferring them to a wire rack to cool completely.

These oatmeal raisin cookies are a delightful blend of chewy and sweet, with a hint of spice from the cinnamon. They're like little bites of comfort, perfect for a cozy afternoon snack or a sweet treat with a glass of milk. Baking them fills your kitchen with a warm, inviting aroma that's hard to resist!

Pita Chips with Hummus

Ingredients for Pita Chips:

- 4 pita bread rounds
- 1/4 cup olive oil
- 1/2 teaspoon garlic powder
- Salt, to taste

Ingredients for Hummus:

- 1 can (15 oz) chickpeas, drained and rinsed
- 1/4 cup tahini (sesame paste)
- 2 tablespoons lemon juice
- 2 cloves garlic, minced
- 1/4 cup olive oil
- Salt and pepper, to taste
- Optional: paprika or chopped parsley for garnish

Instructions:

1. **Make Pita Chips:** Preheat the oven to 375°F (190°C). Cut the pita bread into triangles and place them on a baking sheet. Brush each pita triangle with olive oil and sprinkle with garlic powder and salt. Bake for 10-12 minutes, or until crisp and golden.
2. **Prepare Hummus:** In a food processor, blend the chickpeas, tahini, lemon juice, garlic, and olive oil until smooth. Add a little water if the hummus is too thick. Season with salt and pepper to taste.
3. **Serve:** Transfer the hummus to a serving bowl. Sprinkle with paprika or chopped parsley if desired. Serve with the freshly baked pita chips.

These homemade pita chips paired with creamy hummus make for a delightful snack that's both healthy and satisfying. Each crunchy chip dipped in smooth hummus is a perfect blend of flavors and textures. It's a snack that's not only easy to make but also great for sharing at gatherings or enjoying solo!

Nutella and Banana Sandwich

Ingredients:

- 2 slices of bread (white or whole grain)
- 2-3 tablespoons Nutella (chocolate hazelnut spread)
- 1 ripe banana, sliced
- Butter (optional, for toasting)

Instructions:

1. **Spread Nutella:** Lay out the two slices of bread on a flat surface. Spread a generous layer of Nutella on one side of each slice.
2. **Add Banana:** Arrange the banana slices on top of the Nutella on one of the bread slices.
3. **Assemble Sandwich:** Place the second slice of bread, Nutella side down, on top of the banana slices to form a sandwich.
4. **Optional Toasting:** If you prefer a warm, crispy sandwich, butter the outside of the sandwich and toast it in a skillet over medium heat. Cook until each side is golden brown and the Nutella is slightly melted.
5. **Serve:** Cut the sandwich in half or quarters, depending on your preference, and serve immediately.

This Nutella and banana sandwich is a decadent treat that combines the rich, chocolatey goodness of Nutella with the natural sweetness of banana. It's like a dessert and a snack all in one, perfect for satisfying your sweet tooth at any time of the day!

Fruit Popsicles

Ingredients:

- 2 cups of mixed fresh fruit (such as berries, kiwi, mango, and pineapple), chopped
- 1/2 cup of fruit juice (like apple, orange, or grape juice)
- Optional: 2 tablespoons honey or agave syrup for added sweetness

Instructions:

1. **Prepare the Fruit:** Wash and chop the fruit into small pieces. If you're using larger fruits like mango or pineapple, make sure they're cut small enough to fit into your popsicle molds.
2. **Fill the Molds:** Distribute the mixed fruit evenly into popsicle molds. Try to pack in a variety of colors and types of fruit in each mold for a visually appealing popsicle.
3. **Add Juice:** Pour the fruit juice into each mold to fill the spaces around the fruit. If you're adding honey or agave syrup for sweetness, mix it with the juice before pouring.
4. **Insert Sticks:** Place the popsicle sticks into the molds. If your molds have a cover with built-in sticks, place the cover on top.
5. **Freeze:** Place the molds in the freezer and freeze for at least 4-6 hours, or until the popsicles are completely solid.
6. **Serve:** To release the popsicles, run warm water over the outside of the molds for a few seconds. Gently pull the popsicles out and enjoy.

These fruit popsicles are like a frozen rainbow of natural sweetness. They're not only a fun and refreshing way to cool down on a hot day but also a great opportunity to enjoy a variety of fruits in a single treat. Each lick is a burst of fruity flavor, making them a hit with both kids and adults alike!

Cheese Quesadillas

Ingredients:

- 4 large flour tortillas
- 2 cups shredded cheese (cheddar, Monterey Jack, or a mix)
- Optional fillings: sliced jalapeños, diced bell peppers, onions, or cooked chicken
- Butter or oil for cooking
- Salsa, sour cream, or guacamole for serving

Instructions:

1. **Prepare the Tortillas:** Lay out the tortillas on a flat surface. Sprinkle an even layer of cheese over one half of each tortilla. If using any optional fillings, add them on top of the cheese.
2. **Fold the Tortillas:** Fold the other half of the tortilla over the cheese and fillings to form a half-moon shape.
3. **Cook the Quesadillas:** Heat a little butter or oil in a skillet over medium heat. Place a quesadilla in the skillet and cook until the bottom is golden brown, about 2-3 minutes. Flip it over and cook until the other side is golden brown and the cheese is melted.
4. **Serve:** Remove the quesadilla from the skillet and cut it into wedges. Repeat with the remaining quesadillas.
5. **Serve with Dips**: Serve the quesadillas with salsa, sour cream, or guacamole on the side.

Cheese quesadillas are the ultimate comfort food that's quick and easy to make. They're like a warm, cheesy embrace in every bite, perfect for a quick snack or a casual meal. You can get creative with fillings, making each quesadilla a new flavor adventure!

Chocolate Chip Cookies

Ingredients:

- 2 1/4 cups all-purpose flour
- 1 teaspoon baking soda
- 1 teaspoon salt
- 1 cup (2 sticks) unsalted butter, softened
- 3/4 cup granulated sugar
- 3/4 cup packed brown sugar
- 1 teaspoon vanilla extract
- 2 large eggs
- 2 cups semisweet chocolate chips
- Optional: 1 cup chopped nuts

Instructions:

1. **Combine Dry Ingredients:** In a small bowl, whisk together the flour, baking soda, and salt. Set aside.
2. **Cream Butter and Sugars:** In a large bowl, beat the softened butter, granulated sugar, brown sugar, and vanilla extract until creamy and well combined.
3. **Add Eggs:** Beat in the eggs one at a time, ensuring each egg is fully incorporated before adding the next.
4. **Mix in Dry Ingredients:** Gradually blend in the dry ingredient mixture until just combined. Do not overmix.
5. **Stir in Chocolate Chips:** Fold in the chocolate chips (and nuts, if using) until evenly distributed throughout the dough.
6. **Preheat the Oven:** Preheat your oven to 375°F (190°C). Line baking sheets with parchment paper.
7. **Form Cookie Dough Balls:** Drop rounded tablespoons of dough onto the prepared baking sheets, spacing them about 2 inches apart.
8. **Bake:** Bake in the preheated oven for 9-11 minutes or until the edges are golden brown but the centers are still soft.
9. **Cool:** Remove from the oven and let the cookies cool on the baking sheets for a few minutes before transferring them to wire racks to cool completely.

These chocolate chip cookies are a classic treat that never fails to delight. Each cookie is a perfect blend of buttery dough and melty chocolate chips, creating a comforting and nostalgic experience with every bite. Whether you're baking for a special occasion or just a casual treat, they're sure to bring smiles all around!

Homemade Lemonade

Ingredients:

- 1 cup fresh lemon juice (about 4-6 lemons)
- 1 cup granulated sugar
- 5 cups water, divided
- Ice cubes
- Lemon slices and mint leaves for garnish

Instructions:

1. **Make the Syrup:** In a small saucepan, combine the sugar and 1 cup of water. Bring to a simmer over medium heat, stirring until the sugar is completely dissolved. Remove from heat and let it cool. This creates a simple syrup.
2. **Squeeze Lemons:** Squeeze the lemons until you have 1 cup of juice. Strain the juice to remove seeds and pulp if desired.
3. **Combine Lemon Juice and Syrup:** In a large pitcher, mix the fresh lemon juice with the cooled simple syrup.
4. **Add Water:** Stir in the remaining 4 cups of water. Adjust the water to taste, depending on how sweet or tart you like your lemonade.
5. **Chill:** Refrigerate the lemonade until it's cold or serve immediately over ice cubes.
6. **Garnish and Serve:** Garnish each glass with a slice of lemon and a sprig of mint before serving.

This homemade lemonade is the epitome of refreshing. It's a perfect balance of sweet and tangy flavors, ideal for hot summer days, picnics, or just a relaxing afternoon. Each sip is like a splash of sunshine in your glass, sure to brighten up your day!

Mini Vegetable Spring Rolls

Ingredients:

- 1 tablespoon vegetable oil
- 2 cloves garlic, minced
- 1 cup shredded cabbage
- 1/2 cup grated carrots
- 1/2 cup thinly sliced bell peppers
- 1/4 cup chopped green onions
- 2 tablespoons soy sauce
- 1 teaspoon sesame oil
- Salt and pepper, to taste
- 10-12 spring roll wrappers
- Vegetable oil for frying
- Optional: dipping sauce like sweet chili sauce or soy sauce

Instructions:

1. **Sauté Vegetables:** In a large skillet, heat 1 tablespoon of vegetable oil over medium heat. Add garlic and sauté for a minute. Add cabbage, carrots, bell peppers, and green onions. Cook for 2-3 minutes until the vegetables are softened.
2. **Season:** Add soy sauce and sesame oil to the vegetables. Stir well to combine. Season with salt and pepper. Let the mixture cool down.
3. **Prepare Spring Roll Wrappers:** Work with one wrapper at a time, keeping the others covered with a damp cloth to prevent drying out. Place a wrapper on a clean, dry surface.
4. **Assemble Spring Rolls:** Place a small amount of the vegetable filling near the bottom corner of the wrapper. Fold the sides inward and then roll the wrapper tightly around the filling.
5. **Fry Spring Rolls:** Heat vegetable oil in a deep fryer or large skillet. Fry the spring rolls in batches until golden brown and crispy, about 2-3 minutes per side. Drain on paper towels.
6. **Serve:** Serve the mini vegetable spring rolls hot with dipping sauce on the side.

These mini vegetable spring rolls are like crispy little parcels bursting with fresh flavors. They're a delightful appetizer or snack, perfect for sharing at parties or enjoying as a tasty treat. Dipping them into your favorite sauce adds an extra layer of deliciousness to each bite!

Peanut Butter and Banana Toast

Ingredients:

- 2 slices of bread (whole grain or your choice)
- 2-3 tablespoons peanut butter
- 1 ripe banana, sliced
- Optional: honey, cinnamon, or chia seeds for topping

Instructions:

1. **Toast the Bread:** Toast the bread slices to your desired level of crispiness in a toaster or on a skillet.
2. **Spread Peanut Butter:** Once the bread is toasted, spread a generous layer of peanut butter on each slice.
3. **Add Banana:** Arrange the banana slices over the peanut butter on each slice of bread.
4. **Optional Toppings:** Drizzle with honey, sprinkle with cinnamon, or scatter a few chia seeds over the banana slices for added flavor and nutrition.
5. **Serve:** Enjoy the peanut butter and banana toast immediately while the bread is still warm.

Peanut butter and banana toast is a classic combination that's both nutritious and delicious. It's a quick and easy way to start your day or for a mid-day snack that satisfies. The creamy peanut butter and sweet banana make each bite a delightful experience – it's like a simple joy on a plate!

Homemade Iced Tea

Ingredients:

- 4-6 tea bags (black, green, or herbal tea depending on preference)
- 8 cups of water
- 1/2 cup sugar (adjust to taste)
- Lemon slices (for serving)
- Mint leaves (for garnish)
- Ice cubes

Instructions:

1. **Boil Water:** Bring 4 cups of water to a boil in a large pot.
2. **Steep Tea**: Remove the pot from heat and add the tea bags. Let them steep for about 5-10 minutes, depending on how strong you like your tea.
3. **Remove Tea Bags:** After steeping, remove the tea bags from the water.
4. **Sweeten the Tea:** While the tea is still warm, stir in the sugar until it's completely dissolved. Adjust the amount of sugar according to your taste.
5. **Add Cold Water:** Add the remaining 4 cups of cold water to the tea. This helps cool it down more quickly.
6. **Chill:** Transfer the tea to a pitcher and refrigerate until it's completely chilled.
7. **Serve:** Fill glasses with ice cubes, pour the chilled tea over the ice, and garnish with lemon slices and mint leaves.
8. **Enjoy:** Refresh yourself with a glass of homemade iced tea, perfect for sipping on a warm day.

Homemade iced tea is like a refreshing breeze in a glass. It's a simple, classic beverage that's infinitely customizable – whether you prefer it sweet, tangy with lemon, or minty fresh. There's nothing quite like a tall glass of iced tea to quench your thirst and lift your spirits!

Chocolate Brownies

Ingredients:

- 1/2 cup unsalted butter
- 1 cup granulated sugar
- 2 large eggs
- 1 teaspoon vanilla extract
- 1/3 cup unsweetened cocoa powder
- 1/2 cup all-purpose flour
- 1/4 teaspoon salt
- 1/4 teaspoon baking powder
- Optional: 1/2 cup chopped walnuts or chocolate chips

Instructions:

1. **Preheat the Oven:** Preheat your oven to 350°F (175°C). Grease a 9-inch square baking pan or line it with parchment paper.
2. **Melt Butter:** Melt the butter in a medium saucepan or in the microwave. Once melted, remove from heat.
3. **Mix Wet Ingredients:** Add sugar, eggs, and vanilla extract to the melted butter. Stir well until the mixture is smooth.
4. **Add Dry Ingredients:** Sift in the cocoa powder, flour, salt, and baking powder. Stir until just combined. Avoid overmixing.
5. **Optional Add-Ins:** If using, fold in chopped walnuts or chocolate chips.
6. **Pour into Pan:** Spread the batter evenly into the prepared baking pan.
7. **Bake:** Bake in the preheated oven for 20-25 minutes, or until a toothpick inserted in the center comes out with a few moist crumbs. Be careful not to overbake.
8. **Cool and Serve:** Allow the brownies to cool in the pan before cutting them into squares.

These chocolate brownies are a slice of heaven for chocolate lovers. They're rich, fudgy, and loaded with chocolatey goodness. Perfect for satisfying your sweet tooth, these brownies are great for sharing, gifting, or indulging in a little self-care treat!

Baked Apple Slices with Cinnamon

Ingredients:

- 4 apples, cored and thinly sliced
- 2 tablespoons unsalted butter, melted
- 2 tablespoons brown sugar
- 1 teaspoon ground cinnamon
- A pinch of nutmeg (optional)
- Cooking spray or parchment paper for the baking sheet

Instructions:

1. **Preheat the Oven:** Preheat your oven to 375°F (190°C). Line a baking sheet with cooking spray or parchment paper.
2. **Prepare the Apples:** Core and thinly slice the apples. Place them in a large bowl.
3. **Season the Apples:** Drizzle the melted butter over the apple slices. Add brown sugar, cinnamon, and a pinch of nutmeg if using. Toss everything together until the apple slices are evenly coated with the mixture.
4. **Arrange the Apple Slices:** Spread the apple slices in a single layer on the prepared baking sheet, making sure they don't overlap.
5. **Bake:** Place the baking sheet in the oven and bake for 20-25 minutes, or until the apples are soft and slightly caramelized.
6. **Serve:** Enjoy the baked apple slices as a warm snack, dessert, or even as a topping for oatmeal or yogurt.

These baked apple slices with cinnamon are like a cozy, aromatic delight straight from your oven. They fill your home with the sweet scents of cinnamon and apple, creating a comforting atmosphere. Each bite is a perfect balance of sweetness and spice, making it a healthy treat that feels like indulgence!

Frozen Yogurt Bark

Ingredients:

- 2 cups Greek yogurt (plain or flavored)
- 1/4 cup honey or maple syrup (adjust to taste)
- 1/2 cup mixed berries (such as strawberries, blueberries, raspberries)
- 1/4 cup granola
- Optional toppings: chocolate chips, nuts, seeds, dried fruits, coconut flakes

Instructions:

1. **Prepare the Base:** In a bowl, mix the Greek yogurt with honey or maple syrup. Adjust the sweetness according to your taste.
2. **Line a Baking Sheet:** Line a baking sheet with parchment paper.
3. Spread Yogurt Mixture: Pour the yogurt mixture onto the lined baking sheet and spread it out to about 1/2 inch thickness.
4. **Add Toppings:** Sprinkle the mixed berries and granola evenly over the yogurt. Add any other toppings of your choice like chocolate chips, nuts, seeds, dried fruits, or coconut flakes.
5. **Freeze:** Place the baking sheet in the freezer and freeze the yogurt mixture until it is completely solid, about 3-4 hours or overnight.
6. **Break into Pieces:** Once frozen, break or cut the yogurt bark into pieces.
7. **Serve:** Enjoy the frozen yogurt bark as a refreshing snack. Store any leftovers in the freezer in an airtight container.

Frozen yogurt bark is a playful and versatile treat that's both healthy and satisfying. It's like a customizable canvas where you can get creative with your favorite toppings. Each piece offers a delightful crunch and a burst of flavors, making it a perfect cool treat for any time of the day!

DINNER

Spaghetti Carbonara

Ingredients:

- 400g spaghetti
- 150g pancetta or bacon, diced
- 2 large eggs
- 1 cup grated Parmesan cheese
- 2 cloves garlic, minced
- Salt and black pepper, to taste
- Optional: chopped parsley for garnish

Instructions:

1. **Cook the Pasta:** Bring a large pot of salted water to a boil. Add the spaghetti and cook according to package instructions until al dente. Reserve about 1 cup of pasta water before draining.
2. **Cook Pancetta or Bacon:** While the pasta is cooking, heat a large skillet over medium heat. Add the pancetta or bacon and cook until it is crispy. Add the minced garlic and cook for another minute. Remove from heat.
3. **Prepare the Sauce:** In a bowl, whisk together the eggs and grated Parmesan cheese. Season with black pepper.
4. **Combine Pasta and Pancetta:** Add the drained spaghetti to the skillet with the pancetta and garlic. Toss to combine, making sure the pasta is coated in the fat.
5. **Add Egg Mixture:** Remove the skillet from the heat. Quickly pour the egg and cheese mixture over the hot pasta, stirring vigorously to combine. The residual heat will cook the eggs, creating a creamy sauce. If the sauce is too thick, add some reserved pasta water to reach your desired consistency.
6. **Season and Serve:** Season with salt and black pepper to taste. Garnish with chopped parsley if desired. Serve the spaghetti carbonara immediately.

> **Spaghetti carbonara is a classic Italian dish that's both simple and luxurious. The creamy sauce, crispy pancetta, and al dente pasta create a harmonious blend of flavors and textures. It's like bringing a little piece of Italy to your dinner table - elegant, delicious, and surprisingly easy to make!**

Veggie-Packed Stir Fry

Ingredients:

- 2 tablespoons vegetable oil
- 2 cloves garlic, minced
- 1 tablespoon ginger, minced
- 1 bell pepper, sliced
- 1 carrot, julienned
- 1 cup broccoli florets
- 1/2 cup snap peas
- 1/2 cup baby corn
- 2 green onions, sliced
- 1/4 cup soy sauce
- 1 tablespoon sesame oil
- 1 tablespoon cornstarch mixed with 2 tablespoons water
- Salt and pepper, to taste
- Optional: tofu, chicken, or shrimp for protein
- Optional: sesame seeds, for garnish

Instructions:

1. **Heat the Oil:** In a large skillet or wok, heat the vegetable oil over medium-high heat.
2. **Sauté Garlic and Ginger:** Add the minced garlic and ginger to the skillet. Sauté for about 30 seconds until fragrant.
3. **Cook the Veggies:** Add the sliced bell pepper, julienned carrot, broccoli florets, snap peas, and baby corn. Stir-fry for 5-7 minutes until the vegetables are tender but still crisp.
4. **Add Protein (Optional):** If using tofu, chicken, or shrimp, add it to the skillet and cook until properly heated through or cooked.
5. **Combine Soy Sauce and Sesame Oil:** In a small bowl, mix the soy sauce and sesame oil. Pour this mixture over the stir-fried vegetables.
6. **Thicken the Sauce:** Stir the cornstarch and water mixture into the skillet. Continue to stir-fry until the sauce thickens, about 1-2 minutes.
7. **Season:** Add salt and pepper to taste. Toss in the sliced green onions.
8. **Serve:** Remove from heat and serve the veggie-packed stir fry. Garnish with sesame seeds if desired.

This veggie-packed stir fry is a vibrant and nourishing meal that brings a burst of colors and flavors to your dinner plate. It's a delightful way to enjoy a variety of vegetables, and the quick cooking process keeps everything fresh and crunchy. Each bite is a little adventure in taste and texture, perfect for a healthy yet satisfying meal!

Lemon Butter Fish Fillets

Ingredients:

- 4 fish fillets (such as cod, tilapia, or salmon)
- Salt and pepper, to taste
- 2 tablespoons all-purpose flour (for dusting)
- 4 tablespoons unsalted butter
- 1 lemon, juiced
- 1 tablespoon capers (optional)
- 1 tablespoon fresh parsley, chopped
- Lemon slices, for garnish

Instructions:

1. **Season the Fish:** Pat the fish fillets dry with paper towels. Season both sides with salt and pepper. Lightly dust the fillets with flour, shaking off any excess.
2. **Cook the Fish:** In a large skillet, melt 2 tablespoons of butter over medium-high heat. Add the fish fillets and cook for 3-4 minutes on each side, or until they are golden brown and flake easily with a fork. Remove the fish from the skillet and set aside.
3. **Make Lemon Butter Sauce:** In the same skillet, add the remaining 2 tablespoons of butter, lemon juice, and capers (if using). Stir and cook for a minute, scraping up any browned bits from the bottom of the skillet.
4. **Serve:** Return the fish to the skillet and spoon the lemon butter sauce over the fillets. Sprinkle with chopped parsley.
5. **Garnish:** Serve the fish fillets with lemon slices for garnish.

These lemon butter fish fillets are a light and flavorful dish that's simple to prepare but tastes like gourmet cuisine. The tangy lemon butter sauce complements the delicate fish perfectly, creating a dish that's both refreshing and satisfying. It's like a little taste of the seaside in the comfort of your home!

Chicken Parmesan

Ingredients:

- 4 boneless, skinless chicken breasts
- Salt and pepper, to taste
- 1/2 cup all-purpose flour
- 2 large eggs, beaten
- 1 cup breadcrumbs
- 1/2 cup grated Parmesan cheese
- 2 cups marinara sauce
- 1 cup shredded mozzarella cheese
- 2 tablespoons olive oil
- Fresh basil leaves for garnish

Instructions:

1. **Prepare Chicken:** Preheat your oven to 375°F (190°C). Season the chicken breasts with salt and pepper. Dredge each breast in flour, dip in beaten eggs, and then coat with a mixture of breadcrumbs and grated Parmesan cheese.
2. **Cook Chicken:** In a large skillet, heat olive oil over medium heat. Add the chicken and cook until golden brown on each side, about 3-4 minutes per side. Remove from skillet and place in a baking dish.
3. **Add Sauce and Cheese:** Spoon marinara sauce over each chicken breast, then top with shredded mozzarella cheese.
4. **Bake:** Bake in the preheated oven for 20-25 minutes, or until the chicken is cooked through and the cheese is bubbly and golden.
5. **Garnish and Serve:** Garnish with fresh basil leaves. Serve the Chicken Parmesan with pasta, salad, or your favorite side.

> **Chicken Parmesan is a comforting and satisfying dish that combines tender chicken with a crispy coating, rich tomato sauce, and gooey cheese. It's like enjoying a little piece of Italy right at your dining table, perfect for a family dinner or a special occasion. Each bite is a delightful mix of flavors and textures that's sure to please everyone!**

Beef Stir Fry with Vegetables

Ingredients:

- 400g beef sirloin or flank steak, thinly sliced
- 2 tablespoons soy sauce (for marinade)
- 1 tablespoon cornstarch (for marinade)
- 3 tablespoons vegetable oil
- 1 bell pepper, sliced
- 1 carrot, julienned
- 1 cup broccoli florets
- 1 onion, sliced
- 2 cloves garlic, minced
- 1 tablespoon ginger, minced
- 1/4 cup soy sauce (for sauce)
- 2 tablespoons oyster sauce
- 1 teaspoon sugar
- 1/2 cup water or beef broth
- Salt and pepper, to taste
- Optional: sesame seeds or green onions for garnish

Instructions:

1. **Marinate the Beef:** In a bowl, mix together 2 tablespoons of soy sauce and cornstarch. Add the sliced beef and toss to coat. Let it marinate for at least 15 minutes.
2. **Prepare Stir Fry Sauce:** In a small bowl, combine 1/4 cup soy sauce, oyster sauce, sugar, and water or beef broth. Set aside.
3. **Cook the Beef:** Heat 2 tablespoons of oil in a large skillet or wok over high heat. Add the marinated beef and stir-fry until browned and cooked through. Remove beef from the skillet and set aside.
4. **Stir Fry Vegetables:** Add the remaining 1 tablespoon of oil to the skillet. Add the bell pepper, carrot, broccoli, and onion. Stir-fry for a few minutes until vegetables are tender-crisp. Add the minced garlic and ginger, and stir-fry for another minute.
5. **Combine Beef and Vegetables:** Return the cooked beef to the skillet with the vegetables.
6. **Add Sauce:** Pour the stir fry sauce over the beef and vegetables. Stir well to combine and cook until the sauce thickens slightly.
7. **Season:** Season with salt and pepper to taste.
8. **Garnish and Serve:** Garnish with sesame seeds or chopped green onions if desired. Serve hot with rice or noodles.

This beef stir fry with vegetables is a vibrant and flavorful dish that's both nutritious and satisfying. The combination of tender beef, crisp veggies, and a savory sauce makes it a complete meal that's perfect for a busy weeknight dinner. It's like taking a quick and delicious culinary trip to Asia right from your kitchen!

Spaghetti with Meatballs

Ingredients for Meatballs:

- 500g ground beef
- 1/2 cup breadcrumbs
- 1/4 cup grated Parmesan cheese
- 1 egg
- 2 cloves garlic, minced
- 1 teaspoon dried Italian herbs
- Salt and pepper, to taste

Ingredients for Sauce and Pasta:

- 1 tablespoon olive oil
- 1 onion, chopped
- 2 cloves garlic, minced
- 1 can (28 oz) crushed tomatoes
- 1 teaspoon sugar
- Salt and pepper, to taste
- 400g spaghetti
- Fresh basil leaves for garnish
- Additional grated Parmesan cheese for serving

Instructions:

1. **Make the Meatballs:** In a large bowl, mix together the ground beef, breadcrumbs, Parmesan cheese, egg, minced garlic, Italian herbs, salt, and pepper. Form into small meatballs, about 1 inch in diameter.
2. **Brown the Meatballs:** In a skillet, heat olive oil over medium heat. Add the meatballs and brown them on all sides. Remove from skillet and set aside.
3. **Cook the Sauce:** In the same skillet, add the chopped onion and minced garlic. Cook until the onion is translucent. Stir in the crushed tomatoes and sugar. Season with salt and pepper. Bring to a simmer.
4. **Simmer the Meatballs:** Return the meatballs to the skillet with the tomato sauce. Cover and simmer for about 30 minutes, or until the meatballs are cooked through.
5. **Cook the Spaghetti:** While the meatballs are simmering, cook the spaghetti according to package instructions until al dente. Drain.
6. **Serve:** Serve the meatballs and sauce over the cooked spaghetti. Garnish with fresh basil leaves and sprinkle with additional Parmesan cheese.

Spaghetti with meatballs is a classic Italian-American dish that's hearty and comforting. It's like bringing a little piece of Italy to your dinner table. The savory meatballs, rich tomato sauce, and al dente spaghetti combine for a delicious and satisfying meal that's always a family favorite!

Easy Chicken Curry

Ingredients:

- 4 chicken breasts, cut into bite-sized pieces
- 2 tablespoons vegetable oil
- 1 onion, finely chopped
- 3 cloves garlic, minced
- 1 tablespoon ginger, minced
- 2 tablespoons curry powder
- 1 can (14 oz) coconut milk
- 1 can (14 oz) diced tomatoes
- 1 teaspoon sugar
- Salt and pepper, to taste
- Fresh cilantro, chopped (for garnish)
- Cooked rice, for serving

Instructions:

1. **Cook Chicken:** In a large skillet, heat 1 tablespoon of oil over medium heat. Add the chicken pieces and season with salt and pepper. Cook until browned and cooked through. Remove chicken from the skillet and set aside.
2. **Sauté Aromatics**: In the same skillet, add the remaining tablespoon of oil. Sauté the onion, garlic, and ginger until the onion is soft and translucent.
3. **Add Curry Powder:** Stir in the curry powder and cook for another minute until fragrant.
4. **Add Coconut Milk and Tomatoes:** Pour in the coconut milk and diced tomatoes (with their juice). Stir to combine.
5. **Simmer:** Return the chicken to the skillet. Add the sugar, and season with additional salt and pepper. Bring the mixture to a simmer, then reduce the heat and let it cook for about 20 minutes, or until the sauce thickens slightly.
6. **Garnish and Serve:** Garnish the curry with chopped fresh cilantro. Serve over cooked rice.

Fun Tip: This easy chicken curry is a wonderfully aromatic and flavorful dish that's perfect for a cozy night in. The combination of tender chicken, rich coconut milk, and warming spices creates a comforting and satisfying meal that's both simple to make and a joy to eat. It's like a hug in a bowl, bringing a touch of exotic flair to your dinner routine!

Baked Salmon with Dill

Ingredients:

- 4 salmon fillets
- 2 tablespoons olive oil
- 1 lemon, juiced and zested
- 2 cloves garlic, minced
- 2 tablespoons fresh dill, chopped
- Salt and pepper, to taste
- Lemon slices and extra dill for garnish

Instructions:

1. **Preheat the Oven:** Preheat your oven to 400°F (200°C). Line a baking sheet with parchment paper or lightly grease it.
2. **Prepare the Marinade:** In a small bowl, mix together the olive oil, lemon juice and zest, minced garlic, and chopped dill. Season with salt and pepper.
3. **Marinate the Salmon:** Place the salmon fillets on the prepared baking sheet. Spoon the marinade over the salmon, making sure each fillet is well coated. Let it sit for about 10-15 minutes.
4. **Bake the Salmon:** Place the baking sheet in the oven and bake the salmon for 12-15 minutes, or until the salmon is cooked through and flakes easily with a fork.
5. **Garnish and Serve:** Remove from the oven and garnish with lemon slices and additional fresh dill. Serve the baked salmon warm.

Baked salmon with dill is a dish that's both elegant and easy to prepare. The fresh flavors of lemon and dill complement the richness of the salmon beautifully, creating a meal that feels special enough for a dinner party yet simple enough for a weeknight dinner. It's like bringing a bit of gourmet into your everyday cooking!

Homemade Cheeseburgers

Ingredients:

- 4 hamburger buns
- 1 pound ground beef
- Salt and pepper, to taste
- 4 slices of cheese (cheddar, Swiss, or American)
- Lettuce leaves
- Tomato slices
- Red onion slices
- Ketchup, mustard, and mayonnaise, for serving
- Pickles, for serving
- 1 tablespoon vegetable oil, for cooking

Instructions:

1. **Form the Patties:** Divide the ground beef into 4 equal portions and form each into a patty. Season both sides of the patties with salt and pepper.
2. **Cook the Patties:** Heat a skillet or grill pan over medium-high heat. Add the vegetable oil. Cook the patties for about 3-4 minutes on each side for medium doneness, or until they reach your preferred level of doneness.
3. **Add Cheese:** A minute before the patties are done, place a slice of cheese on top of each patty. Allow the cheese to melt.
4. **Prepare the Buns:** Toast the hamburger buns lightly on the skillet or grill.
5. **Assemble the Burgers:** Spread ketchup, mustard, and mayonnaise on the buns as desired. Place the cheese-topped patties on the bottom halves of the buns. Add lettuce, tomato slices, red onion, and pickles.
6. **Serve:** Top with the other half of the bun and serve the cheeseburgers immediately.

> **Crafting homemade cheeseburgers is a delightful way to bring the classic American diner experience right to your kitchen. The juicy patties, melty cheese, and fresh toppings nestled between toasty buns make for a mouth-watering combination. It's a fun and tasty way to enjoy a casual meal, whether it's a family dinner or a backyard barbecue!**

Veggie Lasagna

Ingredients:

- 9-12 lasagna noodles
- 2 tablespoons olive oil
- 1 onion, chopped
- 3 cloves garlic, minced
- 1 zucchini, sliced
- 1 bell pepper, chopped
- 1 cup mushrooms, sliced
- 1 cup spinach, chopped
- 1 jar (24 oz) marinara sauce
- 2 cups ricotta cheese
- 1 egg
- 1/2 cup grated Parmesan cheese
- 2 cups shredded mozzarella cheese
- Salt and pepper, to taste
- Optional: fresh basil or oregano for seasoning

Instructions:

1. **Cook Lasagna Noodles:** Cook the lasagna noodles according to package instructions until al dente. Drain and set aside.
2. **Sauté Vegetables:** Heat olive oil in a large skillet over medium heat. Sauté onion and garlic until soft. Add zucchini, bell pepper, and mushrooms, cooking until tender. Stir in spinach until wilted. Season with salt, pepper, and optional herbs. Set aside.
3. **Prepare Cheese Mixture**: In a bowl, mix together ricotta cheese, egg, and Parmesan cheese. Season with a little salt and pepper.
4. **Preheat Oven:** Preheat your oven to 375°F (190°C).
5. **Assemble Lasagna:** Spread a thin layer of marinara sauce on the bottom of a baking dish. Layer with lasagna noodles, half of the vegetable mixture, half of the ricotta mixture, and a third of the mozzarella cheese. Repeat layers. Top with a final layer of noodles, marinara sauce, and remaining mozzarella cheese.
6. **Bake:** Cover the lasagna with foil and bake for 25 minutes. Remove the foil and bake for an additional 25 minutes, or until the cheese is bubbly and golden.
7. **Cool and Serve:** Let the lasagna cool for 10-15 minutes before slicing. Serve warm.

This veggie lasagna is a delightful twist on a classic dish, packed with flavors and nutritious ingredients. Each layer unveils a colorful array of vegetables, creamy ricotta, and melted mozzarella, making it not just a meal but a celebration of textures and tastes. It's a comforting and satisfying dish that's sure to please both vegetarians and meat lovers alike!

Sausage and Peppers

Ingredients:

- 4 Italian sausages (pork, chicken, or turkey)
- 2 bell peppers, sliced (use different colors for variety)
- 1 large onion, sliced
- 2 tablespoons olive oil
- 2 cloves garlic, minced
- 1 teaspoon dried oregano or Italian seasoning
- Salt and pepper, to taste
- Optional: red pepper flakes for heat
- Optional: hoagie rolls or crusty bread for serving

Instructions:

1. **Cook the Sausages:** In a large skillet over medium heat, cook the sausages until browned on all sides and cooked through, about 10-15 minutes. Remove from the skillet and set aside.
2. **Sauté Vegetables: In** the same skillet, add the olive oil, followed by the sliced bell peppers and onion. Sauté until the vegetables are soft and slightly caramelized, about 8-10 minutes.
3. **Add Flavor:** Add the minced garlic, oregano or Italian seasoning, and red pepper flakes if using. Cook for another 1-2 minutes until fragrant.
4. **Combine Sausages and Vegetables:** Slice the cooked sausages into bite-sized pieces and return them to the skillet with the peppers and onions. Stir to combine and heat through. Season with salt and pepper.
5. **Serve:** Serve the sausage and peppers mixture hot. You can enjoy it as is, or serve it in hoagie rolls or with crusty bread on the side.

Sausage and peppers is a rustic, hearty dish that's bursting with flavors. The juicy sausages and sweet, tender peppers create a perfect harmony in each bite. It's a simple yet satisfying meal that's great for a quick dinner, a family gathering, or even as a delicious sandwich filling!

Baked Chicken Drumsticks

Ingredients:

- 8 chicken drumsticks
- 2 tablespoons olive oil
- 1 teaspoon garlic powder
- 1 teaspoon onion powder
- 1 teaspoon paprika
- 1/2 teaspoon dried thyme
- Salt and pepper, to taste
- Optional: lemon wedges and fresh parsley for serving

Instructions:

1. **Preheat the Oven:** Preheat your oven to 425°F (220°C). Line a baking sheet with aluminum foil or parchment paper for easy cleanup.
2. **Prepare the Drumsticks:** Pat the chicken drumsticks dry with paper towels. This helps to get a crispy skin.
3. **Season the Chicken:** In a large bowl, mix together the olive oil, garlic powder, onion powder, paprika, dried thyme, salt, and pepper. Add the drumsticks to the bowl and toss to coat evenly with the seasoning.
4. **Arrange on Baking Sheet:** Place the seasoned drumsticks on the prepared baking sheet, making sure they are not touching each other.
5. **Bake:** Bake in the preheated oven for 35-45 minutes, or until the drumsticks are golden brown and the internal temperature reaches 165°F (74°C).
6. **Serve:** Let the drumsticks rest for a few minutes before serving. Serve with lemon wedges and garnish with fresh parsley if desired.

These baked chicken drumsticks are a delicious and easy way to enjoy a classic favorite. The mix of spices gives a savory and slightly smoky flavor, while baking them creates a wonderfully crispy skin. They're perfect for a family dinner, a casual gathering, or even as a tasty snack during game night!

Creamy Mushroom Risotto

Ingredients:

- 1 cup Arborio rice
- 2 tablespoons olive oil
- 1 small onion, finely chopped
- 2 cloves garlic, minced
- 2 cups mushrooms, sliced (such as button or cremini)
- 4 cups chicken or vegetable broth, kept warm
- 1/2 cup white wine (optional)
- 1/2 cup grated Parmesan cheese
- 2 tablespoons unsalted butter
- Salt and pepper, to taste
- Fresh parsley, chopped for garnish

Instructions:

1. **Sauté Aromatics:** In a large skillet or saucepan, heat the olive oil over medium heat. Add the onion and garlic, sautéing until the onion is translucent.
2. **Cook Mushrooms:** Add the sliced mushrooms to the skillet and cook until they are soft and browned.
3. **Toast the Rice:** Stir in the Arborio rice, coating it with the oil and cooking until the edges become slightly translucent, about 2 minutes.
4. **Add Liquid:** Pour in the white wine, if using, and let it simmer until it's mostly absorbed. Then, add the warm broth one ladle at a time, stirring constantly and allowing the rice to absorb the liquid before adding more.
5. **Continue Cooking:** Keep adding broth and stirring the risotto. This process should take about 18-20 minutes. The rice should be al dente and the mixture creamy.
6. **Finish the Risotto:** Remove the skillet from heat. Stir in the butter and grated Parmesan cheese until well combined. Season with salt and pepper to taste.
7. **Garnish and Serve:** Serve the risotto warm, garnished with chopped parsley and additional Parmesan cheese if desired.

Creamy mushroom risotto is a luxurious and comforting dish that's perfect for a cozy evening. The creamy texture of the rice combined with the earthy flavor of mushrooms creates a symphony of flavors. Each spoonful is a delightful experience, showcasing the simple elegance of Italian cooking!

Shepherd's Pie

Ingredients:

- 1 pound ground lamb or beef
- 1 onion, diced
- 2 carrots, diced
- 2 cloves garlic, minced
- 1 cup frozen peas
- 2 tablespoons tomato paste
- 1 cup beef or chicken broth
- 1 teaspoon Worcestershire sauce
- Salt and pepper, to taste
- 3 cups mashed potatoes (prepared in advance)
- 1/2 cup grated cheddar cheese (optional)

Instructions:

1. **Cook the Meat:** Preheat your oven to 375°F (190°C). In a large skillet, cook the ground lamb or beef over medium heat until browned. Drain excess fat.
2. **Sauté Vegetables:** Add the diced onion, carrots, and minced garlic to the skillet with the meat. Cook until the vegetables are softened.
3. **Add Peas and Seasonings:** Stir in the frozen peas, tomato paste, and Worcestershire sauce. Pour in the broth and bring the mixture to a simmer. Season with salt and pepper. Simmer for about 10 minutes, or until the liquid reduces slightly.
4. **Prepare Baking Dish:** Spoon the meat and vegetable mixture into a baking dish, spreading it into an even layer.
5. **Add Mashed Potatoes:** Spoon the mashed potatoes over the top of the meat mixture. Use a fork to create ridges on the surface. Sprinkle with grated cheddar cheese if using.
6. **Bake:** Place the baking dish in the oven and bake for 20-25 minutes, or until the mashed potatoes are golden brown and the edges are bubbling.
7. **Serve:** Let the shepherd's pie cool for a few minutes before serving.

Shepherd's pie is a hearty and comforting dish that's perfect for a wholesome family meal. The savory meat and vegetable base topped with creamy mashed potatoes make for a delightful combination of textures and flavors. It's a rustic, satisfying meal that feels like a warm hug on a plate!

Ratatouille

Ingredients:

- 1 eggplant, sliced into rounds
- 2 zucchinis, sliced into rounds
- 2 yellow squashes, sliced into rounds
- 2 bell peppers (any color), sliced
- 4 tomatoes, sliced
- 1 onion, thinly sliced
- 4 cloves garlic, minced
- 1/4 cup olive oil
- 1 teaspoon dried thyme
- Salt and pepper, to taste
- Optional: fresh basil or parsley for garnish

Instructions:

1. **Prepare Vegetables:** Preheat your oven to 375°F (190°C). Slice the eggplant, zucchinis, yellow squashes, bell peppers, and tomatoes into round slices. Thinly slice the onion and mince the garlic.
2. **Sauté Onion and Garlic:** In a large skillet, heat 2 tablespoons of olive oil over medium heat. Add the onion and garlic and sauté until softened.
3. **Arrange Vegetables:** In a large baking dish, spread the sautéed onion and garlic as the first layer. Then, arrange the sliced vegetables (eggplant, zucchinis, yellow squashes, bell peppers, and tomatoes) in an alternating pattern (like shingles) on top of the onion layer.
4. **Season:** Drizzle the remaining olive oil over the vegetables. Sprinkle with dried thyme, salt, and pepper.
5. **Bake:** Cover the dish with aluminum foil and bake in the preheated oven for about 40 minutes. Then, uncover and bake for another 20 minutes or until the vegetables are tender and lightly browned.
6. **Garnish and Serve:** Garnish with fresh basil or parsley before serving. Serve the ratatouille warm as a side dish or a main course.

Ratatouille is a colorful and flavorful dish that celebrates the simplicity and elegance of vegetables. This classic French recipe transforms humble ingredients into a vibrant and tasty dish, perfect for impressing guests or enjoying a healthy meal. Each bite is a delightful blend of textures and Mediterranean flavors!

Tofu and Broccoli Stir Fry

Ingredients:

- 1 block (14 oz) firm tofu, drained and cut into cubes
- 2 cups broccoli florets
- 2 tablespoons vegetable oil
- 2 cloves garlic, minced
- 1 tablespoon ginger, minced
- 1/4 cup soy sauce
- 2 tablespoons brown sugar
- 1 tablespoon cornstarch
- 1/2 cup water
- Salt and pepper, to taste
- Optional: sesame seeds or green onions for garnish

Instructions:

1. **Prepare the Tofu:** Press the tofu to remove excess moisture, then cut it into bite-sized cubes. Season with a little salt and pepper.
2. **Cook the Tofu:** In a large skillet or wok, heat 1 tablespoon of oil over medium-high heat. Add the tofu and fry until all sides are golden brown. Remove the tofu from the skillet and set aside.
3. **Cook the Broccoli:** In the same skillet, add the broccoli florets and a splash of water. Cover and cook for about 3-4 minutes until the broccoli is bright green and tender-crisp. Remove and set aside.
4. **Make the Sauce:** In a small bowl, whisk together soy sauce, brown sugar, cornstarch, and water. Set aside.
5. **Sauté Garlic and Ginger:** Heat the remaining oil in the skillet. Add minced garlic and ginger, and sauté for about 30 seconds until fragrant.
6. **Combine Ingredients:** Return the tofu and broccoli to the skillet. Pour the sauce over the top and stir well to combine. Cook for a few minutes until the sauce thickens.
7. **Garnish and Serve:** Season with salt and pepper to taste. Garnish with sesame seeds or chopped green onions if desired. Serve hot, ideally with rice or noodles.

This tofu and broccoli stir fry is a vibrant and nourishing dish that's full of flavors and textures. The tofu provides a satisfying meatiness, while the broccoli adds a delightful crunch. It's a simple yet delicious way to enjoy a plant-based meal that's both filling and healthy!

Beef Tacos

Ingredients:

- 1 pound ground beef
- 1 tablespoon olive oil
- 1 onion, diced
- 2 cloves garlic, minced
- 1 packet taco seasoning (or 2 tablespoons homemade taco seasoning)
- 8-10 taco shells or small tortillas
- 1 cup shredded lettuce
- 1 tomato, diced
- 1 cup shredded cheddar cheese
- 1/2 cup sour cream
- 1/2 cup salsa
- Optional: jalapeños, cilantro, lime wedges for garnish

Instructions:

1. **Cook the Beef:** Heat the olive oil in a skillet over medium heat. Add the diced onion and minced garlic, sautéing until the onion is translucent.
2. **Add Ground Beef:** Add the ground beef to the skillet. Cook, breaking it apart with a spatula, until it's fully browned and cooked through.
3. **Add Seasoning:** Drain any excess fat from the skillet. Stir in the taco seasoning and cook according to the packet's instructions (usually adding a bit of water and simmering for a few minutes).
4. **Prepare Toppings:** While the beef is cooking, prepare the toppings: shred the lettuce, dice the tomato, and shred the cheese.
5. **Warm the Shells:** Warm the taco shells or tortillas in the oven or on a skillet, according to package instructions.
6. **Assemble the Tacos:** Spoon the cooked beef into the taco shells or tortillas. Top with lettuce, tomato, cheese, sour cream, and salsa.
7. **Garnish:** Add jalapeños, cilantro, and a squeeze of lime if desired.
8. **Serve:** Serve the beef tacos immediately, allowing everyone to build their own perfect taco.

> **Beef tacos are a fun and versatile dish that's perfect for a casual dinner or a get-together. Everyone can customize their taco with their favorite toppings, making it a delightful and interactive meal. It's like having a mini fiesta on your dinner table!**

Chicken Fajitas

Ingredients:

- 3 chicken breasts, thinly sliced
- 2 bell peppers (different colors), sliced
- 1 large onion, sliced
- 2 tablespoons olive oil
- 1 tablespoon chili powder
- 1 teaspoon cumin
- 1 teaspoon paprika
- 1/2 teaspoon garlic powder
- Salt and pepper, to taste
- Juice of 1 lime
- 8-10 small flour tortillas
- Optional garnishes: sour cream, avocado, shredded cheese, salsa, lime wedges

Instructions:

1. **Marinate the Chicken:** In a bowl, combine the chili powder, cumin, paprika, garlic powder, salt, and pepper. Add the chicken slices and toss to coat evenly. Drizzle with the juice of half the lime and set aside to marinate for at least 15 minutes.
2. **Cook the Chicken:** In a large skillet or frying pan, heat 1 tablespoon of olive oil over medium-high heat. Add the chicken and cook until browned and cooked through. Remove the chicken from the skillet and set aside.
3. **Sauté Vegetables:** In the same skillet, add the remaining tablespoon of olive oil. Sauté the sliced bell peppers and onion until they are soft and slightly caramelized.
4. **Combine Chicken and Vegetables:** Return the chicken to the skillet with the vegetables. Squeeze the remaining lime juice over the top and stir to combine.
5. **Warm the Tortillas:** Heat the tortillas in a dry skillet, microwave, or oven until they are warm and pliable.
6. **Assemble the Fajitas:** Spoon the chicken and vegetable mixture into the warm tortillas.
7. **Add Garnishes:** Top with your choice of garnishes like sour cream, avocado, shredded cheese, or salsa.
8. **Serve:** Roll up the tortillas and serve the fajitas hot, with lime wedges on the side for extra zing.

Chicken fajitas are a sizzling and colorful dish that's sure to impress. The combination of spiced, juicy chicken with sweet, sautéed bell peppers and onions, all wrapped in a soft tortilla, creates a delightful meal that's both tasty and fun to eat. It's like bringing the excitement of a Mexican restaurant to your own dining table!

Margherita Pizza

Ingredients:

- Pizza dough (store-bought or homemade)
- 1/2 cup tomato sauce (pizza sauce or crushed tomatoes)
- 2 cups shredded mozzarella cheese
- 2-3 ripe tomatoes, sliced
- Fresh basil leaves
- 1 clove garlic, minced
- 2 tablespoons olive oil
- Salt and pepper, to taste
- Optional: Parmesan cheese for grating

Instructions:

1. **Prepare the Oven:** Preheat your oven to the highest temperature it can go, typically between 450°F (230°C) and 500°F (260°C). If you have a pizza stone, place it in the oven to heat up.
2. **Roll Out the Dough:** On a floured surface, roll out the pizza dough to your desired thickness. Transfer it to a piece of parchment paper for easy transfer to the oven.
3. **Add Sauce and Toppings:** Spread the tomato sauce over the dough, leaving a small border around the edges. Sprinkle the minced garlic over the sauce. Arrange the sliced mozzarella and tomato slices on top. Season with salt and pepper.
4. **Drizzle Olive Oil:** Drizzle olive oil over the pizza toppings.
5. **Bake the Pizza:** Transfer the pizza (on the parchment paper) to the preheated pizza stone or a baking sheet. Bake for 10-15 minutes, or until the crust is golden and the cheese is bubbly and slightly browned.
6. **Add Fresh Basil:** Once the pizza is out of the oven, immediately add fresh basil leaves over the top.
7. **Optional Parmesan:** Grate some Parmesan cheese over the pizza for added flavor, if desired.
8. **Serve:** Slice the pizza and serve it hot.

Margherita pizza is a timeless classic that honors the simplicity and freshness of its ingredients. The combination of tangy tomato sauce, melted mozzarella, and aromatic basil on a crisp crust creates a perfect harmony of flavors. Each bite is a tribute to the art of Italian pizza making – simple, elegant, and utterly delicious!

Roast Chicken with Vegetables

Ingredients:

- 1 whole chicken (about 4-5 pounds)
- 2 tablespoons olive oil
- 2 teaspoons garlic powder
- 1 teaspoon dried thyme
- 1 teaspoon dried rosemary
- Salt and pepper, to taste
- 1 lemon, halved
- 1 onion, quartered
- 3 carrots, cut into chunks
- 3 potatoes, cut into chunks
- Optional: other vegetables like Brussels sprouts or parsnips

Instructions:

1. **Preheat the Oven:** Preheat your oven to 425°F (220°C).
2. **Prepare the Chicken:** Remove the giblets from the chicken and pat it dry with paper towels. Rub the outside of the chicken with 1 tablespoon of olive oil. Season the chicken all over with garlic powder, thyme, rosemary, salt, and pepper.
3. **Stuff the Chicken:** Place the lemon halves and onion quarters inside the cavity of the chicken.
4. **Arrange in Roasting Pan:** Place the chicken in a large roasting pan. Surround it with the chopped carrots, potatoes, and any other vegetables you're using. Drizzle the remaining olive oil over the vegetables and season them with salt and pepper.
5. **Roast the Chicken:** Put the roasting pan in the oven and roast for about 1 hour and 20 minutes, or until the internal temperature of the chicken reaches 165°F (75°C) and the juices run clear.
6. **Rest the Chicken:** Remove the roasting pan from the oven and let the chicken rest for 10-15 minutes before carving. This helps to keep the chicken juicy.
7. **Serve:** Carve the chicken and serve it with the roasted vegetables on the side.

Roast chicken with vegetables is a classic comfort food that's both delicious and heartwarming. The chicken turns out juicy and flavorful, while the vegetables become tender and infused with the chicken's savory juices. It's a complete meal that's perfect for a cozy family dinner or a special occasion, filling your home with delightful aromas!

RECIPES TO MAKE WITH FRIENDS

Mini Homemade Pizzas

Ingredients:

- Pizza dough (store-bought or homemade, divided into small portions)
- Tomato sauce (pizza sauce or marinara)
- Shredded mozzarella cheese
- Assorted toppings: pepperoni slices, diced bell peppers, sliced mushrooms, olives, cooked sausage, red onion, etc.
- Olive oil for brushing
- Optional: Italian seasoning or dried basil for sprinkling
- Optional: grated Parmesan cheese

Instructions:

1. **Preheat the Oven:** Preheat your oven to 450°F (230°C). If you have a pizza stone, place it in the oven to heat.
2. **Prepare Dough:** Divide the pizza dough into small portions, each enough to make a mini pizza. On a floured surface, roll out each portion into a small circle.
3. **Brush with Olive Oil:** Lightly brush the top of each dough circle with olive oil.
4. **Add Sauce and Toppings:** Spread a thin layer of tomato sauce over each mini pizza. Sprinkle shredded mozzarella cheese on top. Arrange your chosen toppings on the cheese.
5. **Optional Seasoning:** Sprinkle a little Italian seasoning or dried basil over the pizzas for added flavor.
6. **Bake the Pizzas:** Place the mini pizzas on a baking sheet or the preheated pizza stone. Bake in the oven for 10-12 minutes, or until the crust is golden and the cheese is bubbly.
7. **Optional Parmesan:** Sprinkle grated Parmesan cheese over the hot pizzas for extra flavor.
8. **Serve:** Serve the mini homemade pizzas hot, allowing everyone to grab their favorite combination.

> **Mini homemade pizzas are a fantastic way to enjoy a fun and interactive cooking experience with friends. Everyone can customize their pizza with their favorite toppings, turning mealtime into a creative and social activity. It's like having a personalized pizza party right at home!**

Build-Your-Own Taco Bar

Ingredients for Taco Bar:

- 2 pounds ground beef or chicken, cooked and seasoned with taco seasoning
- 8-10 flour or corn tortillas, warmed
- Shredded lettuce
- Diced tomatoes
- Sliced jalapeños
- Chopped onions
- Shredded cheddar or Mexican blend cheese
- Sour cream
- Guacamole or diced avocados
- Salsa or pico de gallo
- Lime wedges
- Chopped cilantro
- Optional: black beans or refried beans, corn, olives, bell peppers

Instructions:

1. **Prepare the Meat:** Cook the ground beef or chicken in a skillet over medium heat. Drain any excess grease. Stir in taco seasoning and cook according to package instructions.
2. **Warm the Tortillas:** Heat the tortillas in a dry skillet or microwave until warm and pliable. Keep them warm by wrapping them in a clean towel or placing them in a tortilla warmer.
3. **Arrange the Taco Bar:** Set up a table or counter space with all the taco ingredients. Arrange the cooked meat, tortillas, and all the toppings in separate bowls or platters.
4. **Include Serving Utensils:** Provide serving utensils for each ingredient, along with plates and napkins.
5. **Invite to Assemble:** Invite your friends to build their own tacos by filling a tortilla with their choice of meat, vegetables, cheese, and other toppings.
6. **Enjoy:** Enjoy the fun and interactive experience of making and eating tacos together.

A build-your-own taco bar is the perfect setup for a casual and fun gathering with friends. It allows everyone to tailor their tacos to their own tastes, creating a variety of flavors and combinations. This interactive meal is not just about enjoying delicious food but also about the joy of sharing and customizing your meal together!

Chocolate Fondue with Fruits

Ingredients for Fondue:

- 8 ounces semisweet or dark chocolate, chopped
- 1/2 cup heavy cream
- 2 tablespoons sugar (optional, adjust to taste)
- 1 teaspoon vanilla extract

Ingredients for Dipping:

- Fresh fruits: strawberries, banana slices, apple slices, pineapple chunks
- Other options: marshmallows, pound cake cubes, pretzels

Instructions:

1. **Prepare the Fruits and Dipping Items:** Wash and cut the fruits into bite-sized pieces. Arrange the fruits and other dipping items on a platter.
2. **Make the Fondue:** In a saucepan, heat the heavy cream over low heat until it's warm but not boiling. Add the chopped chocolate and sugar (if using) to the cream. Stir continuously until the chocolate is completely melted and the mixture is smooth. Stir in the vanilla extract.
3. **Transfer to Fondue Pot:** Pour the chocolate mixture into a fondue pot or keep it in the saucepan on low heat. The fondue should be kept warm to maintain a dipping consistency.
4. **Serve:** Place the fondue pot in the center of your serving table, surrounded by the platter of fruits and other items for dipping.
5. **Enjoy:** Use fondue forks or skewers to dip the fruits and other items into the warm chocolate fondue.

> **Chocolate fondue with fruits is a delightful and interactive dessert that's perfect for sharing with friends. Dipping various fruits into the rich, velvety chocolate turns dessert into a fun and social experience. It's like having a little chocolate party where everyone can enjoy their favorite combinations!**

Homemade Sushi Rolls

Ingredients:

- Sushi rice (2 cups of rice cooked with 3 cups of water, cooled and seasoned with sushi vinegar)
- Nori sheets
- Fillings: sliced cucumber, avocado, cooked shrimp, crab meat, smoked salmon, cream cheese
- Soy sauce, for dipping
- Wasabi and pickled ginger, for serving
- Optional: sesame seeds, for garnish

Instructions:

1. **Prepare Sushi Rice:** Cook the sushi rice according to package instructions. Once cooked, transfer to a large bowl. While still warm, gently fold in sushi vinegar. Allow the rice to cool to room temperature.
2. **Prepare the Fillings:** Cut the cucumber, avocado, and your choice of proteins into long, thin strips. Set aside.
3. **Assemble the Sushi Rolls:** Place a nori sheet on a bamboo sushi mat. With wet hands, spread a thin layer of sushi rice onto the nori, leaving about an inch of space at the top.
4. **Add Fillings:** Lay your chosen fillings in a line across the middle of the rice. Don't overfill.
5. **Roll the Sushi:** Lift the edge of the mat closest to you and roll it over the fillings to create a tight roll. Use the mat to shape and tighten the roll. Continue rolling until you reach the end of the nori.
6. **Cut the Sushi:** With a sharp, wet knife, cut the roll into bite-sized pieces. Clean the knife between cuts for cleaner slices.
7. **Serve:** Arrange the sushi on a platter. Sprinkle with sesame seeds if desired. Serve with soy sauce, wasabi, and pickled ginger on the side.

Making homemade sushi rolls is a creative and enjoyable activity, especially when done with friends. It's like a culinary adventure where you can experiment with different fillings and techniques. Enjoy the process of rolling and savoring your custom sushi creations – it's a fun way to explore the art of sushi making!

Pasta Bake Party

Ingredients:

- 1 pound pasta (penne, rigatoni, or similar)
- 1 jar (24 oz) marinara sauce
- 1 cup ricotta cheese
- 2 cups shredded mozzarella cheese
- 1/2 cup grated Parmesan cheese
- 1 tablespoon olive oil
- 2 cloves garlic, minced
- 1 small onion, chopped
- 1 bell pepper, chopped
- 1 zucchini, chopped
- 1 cup mushrooms, sliced
- Salt and pepper, to taste
- Optional: cooked ground beef or Italian sausage
- Optional: red pepper flakes, dried basil, or oregano for extra flavor

Instructions:

1. **Preheat Oven:** Preheat your oven to 375°F (190°C).
2. **Cook Pasta:** Cook the pasta according to package instructions until just al dente. Drain and set aside.
3. **Sauté Vegetables:** In a large skillet, heat olive oil over medium heat. Add garlic, onion, bell pepper, zucchini, and mushrooms. Sauté until vegetables are softened. Season with salt, pepper, and optional spices.
4. **Combine Ingredients:** In a large bowl, mix the cooked pasta, sautéed vegetables, marinara sauce, ricotta cheese, and half of the mozzarella cheese. If using, add cooked ground beef or sausage.
5. **Assemble Pasta Bake:** Transfer the pasta mixture to a greased baking dish. Sprinkle the remaining mozzarella and Parmesan cheese on top.
6. **Bake:** Place in the oven and bake for 20-25 minutes, or until the cheese is melted and bubbly.
7. **Serve:** Let the pasta bake cool for a few minutes before serving. This dish is great for a party where guests can serve themselves a hearty and comforting portion.

Hosting a pasta bake party is a fantastic way to enjoy a cozy and delicious meal with friends. It's a versatile dish that allows for a variety of ingredients, catering to different tastes and preferences. The combination of melted cheese, savory sauce, and pasta makes every bite a delightful experience – it's like a gathering around a table of comfort food joy!

DIY Burger Station

Ingredients for Burger Station:

- Ground beef or alternative (like turkey, chicken, or plant-based patties)
- Burger buns
- Cheese slices (cheddar, Swiss, American, etc.)
- Lettuce leaves
- Tomato slices
- Red onion slices
- Pickles
- Ketchup, mustard, mayonnaise
- BBQ sauce
- Optional toppings: sautéed mushrooms, bacon, avocado slices, jalapeños
- Salt and pepper, for seasoning
- Cooking oil, for grilling

Additional Equipment:

- Grill or skillet
- Spatulas
- Serving plates
- Napkins

Instructions:

1. **Prepare Patties:** Form the ground meat into patties. Season both sides with salt and pepper.
2. **Heat the Grill:** Heat a grill or skillet over medium-high heat. Lightly oil the grate or skillet.
3. **Cook Burgers:** Place the patties on the grill or skillet. Cook for about 3-4 minutes per side for medium-rare, or longer for well-done. In the last minute of cooking, place a cheese slice on each patty to melt.
4. **Toast Buns:** Lightly toast the burger buns on the grill or skillet.
5. **Arrange the Station:** Set up a table with all the burger components. Place the cooked patties, toasted buns, and all the toppings and condiments in an accessible arrangement.
6. **Build Your Burger:** Invite guests to build their own burgers, choosing from the variety of toppings and condiments.
7. **Serve:** Enjoy the fun and interactive experience of making and eating customized burgers.

A DIY burger station is the perfect setup for a fun and interactive meal with friends and family. Everyone gets to be a chef, creating their dream burger with their favorite combinations of toppings and sauces. It's not just about enjoying a delicious burger, but about the joy of customizing your meal and sharing the experience together!

Ice Cream Sundae Bar

Ingredients for Sundae Bar:

- Assorted ice cream flavors (vanilla, chocolate, strawberry, etc.)
- Chocolate syrup
- Caramel sauce
- Whipped cream
- Chopped nuts (almonds, peanuts, walnuts)
- Sprinkles
- Maraschino cherries
- Fresh fruits (banana slices, berries)
- Crushed cookies or candy pieces
- Waffle cones or bowls

Additional Equipment:

- Ice cream scoop
- Serving bowls or cones
- Spoons
- Napkins

Instructions:

1. **Arrange Ice Cream:** Keep the ice cream in the freezer until you're ready to serve to ensure it stays firm. You can set up a cooler with ice to keep the ice cream cold while serving.
2. **Prepare Toppings:** Organize all the toppings in separate bowls. Include a variety of sauces, nuts, sprinkles, fruits, and other sweet treats.
3. **Set Up Serving Station:** Arrange the ice cream, toppings, cones, bowls, and spoons on a large table or counter.
4. **Scoop and Serve:** When ready to serve, scoop the ice cream into bowls or cones. Let your guests choose their favorite flavors and toppings.
5. **Build the Sundaes:** Guests can create their own sundaes by adding their preferred toppings and sauces to their ice cream.
6. **Enjoy:** Have fun mixing and matching flavors and toppings, and enjoy the delicious ice cream sundaes.

An ice cream sundae bar is a delightful treat for any gathering, offering a sweet and interactive dessert experience. Guests of all ages can enjoy customizing their sundaes with a variety of toppings and sauces, turning dessert time into a fun and creative activity. It's like having your own ice cream parlor at home!

CONCLUSION

Your Journey Continues: Beyond the Cookbook

Hey there, awesome young chefs! You've flipped through these pages, tackled some delicious recipes, and have turned your kitchen into a realm of endless possibilities. But guess what? This is just the beginning of your culinary adventure!

Remember, cooking isn't just about following recipes - it's about experimenting, getting creative, and sometimes making a glorious mess (shh, we won't tell if you don't). Each time you cook, you're learning something new, whether it's how to perfectly flip a pancake or discovering that, yes, you can have too much garlic (or can you?).

Don't be afraid to mix things up. Swap out ingredients, try new spices, or invent a completely new dish. Who knows? You might just create the next big hit in your household. And if things don't go as planned, no worries - it's all part of the learning process. Plus, the best stories come from kitchen blunders (ever heard of a chocolate chip cookie? That was an 'oops' that turned out pretty yummy).

Invite your friends over for a cooking party, make dinner for your family, or treat yourself to a homemade snack. Cooking is more than just making food; it's about sharing, caring, and having a ton of fun while you're at it.

And remember, as you continue your journey beyond this cookbook, keep your apron tied, your taste buds ready, and your imagination on full blast. The world of cooking is vast and exciting, filled with flavors to explore and dishes to master. You've got the skills, the smarts, and now the experience to make a splash in the culinary world. Go ahead, chef - the kitchen is your playground!

Keep cooking, keep laughing, and keep savoring every bite. Bon appétit!

SCAN THIS CODE AND GET YOUR BONUS

Printed in Great Britain
by Amazon